# Meeting the Guv'nor

'So many of the men I interview are in the dark world of violence, which is really a form of hell. But Alan Mortlock has found his way out. This is inspirational.'

Kate Kray

# Meeting the Guv'nor

**Alan Mortlock**

**with Greg Watts**

Hodder & Stoughton
LONDON SYDNEY AUCKLAND

Copyright © 2003 by Alan Mortlock and Greg Watts

First published in Great Britain in 2003

The right of Alan Mortlock and Greg Watts to be identified
as the Authors of the Work has been asserted by them in
accordance with the Copyright, Designs and Patents Act 1988.

10 9 8 7 6 5 4 3

British Library Cataloguing in Publication Data
A record for this book is available from the British Library

ISBN 0 340 86145 2

Typeset in Bembo by Avon DataSet Ltd,
Bidford-on-Avon, Warwickshire

Printed and bound in Great Britain by
Bookmarque Ltd, Croydon, Surrey

The paper and board used in this paperback are natural recyclable
products made from wood grown in sustainable forests.
The manufacturing processes conform to the environmental
regulations of the country of origin.

Hodder & Stoughton
A Division of Hodder Headline Ltd
338 Euston Road
London NW1 3BH
www.madaboutbooks.com

To Laura, and my sons, Adam, Jamie, Sean and Mel.

# Contents

# Foreword by Kate Kray

I was introduced to Alan Mortlock by Roy 'prettyboy' Shaw – the ultimate street fighter. Roy suggested I speak to Alan about his fighting ability and his fearsome reputation.

I've interviewed tough guys from all walks of life – terrorists, gangsters, murderers, Yardies, Hell's Angels, Triads – you name 'em – I've interviewed 'em, and they all have a tale to tell. But Alan was different. He is an inspirational character. For seventeen years, violence, drugs and alcohol were his daily bread until, one day, the power of prayer managed to achieve what no amount of crime and punishment could do. In a truly miraculous turnaround, Alan found Jesus, and almost overnight gave up everything he had ever known. He is now a born-again Christian who has found peace and success in his life.

What I find interesting is that he combines two worlds: the macho, testosterone world of unlicensed boxing, and that of Christianity.

So many of the men I interview are in the dark world of violence, which is really a form of hell, but Alan has found his way out, and this is inspirational. After speaking to Alan I felt different. It's hard to explain, and maybe it sounds a bit dramatic, but I felt a sort of calm and at peace with myself. I don't know why or how Alan had that effect on me, but he did.

Kate Kray

# Acknowledgements

I'd like to thank Greg Watts for drawing out my memories, thoughts and feelings over a number of months when he came to see me at my house in Leyton. And I'd like to thank David Moloney at Hodder & Stoughton for deciding to commission this book.

# 1

# The Battle of Ilford

It was a hot Wednesday night in the summer of 1977. I was standing at the bar of the Room at the Top night club in High Road, Ilford, waiting to get served. As there were only twenty minutes to go before chucking out time, people were thronging and pushing around the long, circular bar, waving pound notes and glasses at the bar staff.

The Room at the Top got its name because it was at the top of Harrison's and Gibson's department store. Like many night clubs at that time, it was done out in chrome, glass and velvet and had twinkly lights on the ceiling. It wasn't my favourite place, but tonight was half-price Southern Comfort night, so it was a cheap way of getting drunk.

Along with Tiffanys, on the opposite side of the road, the Room at the Top was one of the most popular venues in the area, attracting people from all over east London and Essex. But the club also had a reputation for attracting troublemakers, and there'd been quite a few fights both inside and outside.

'Oi! What are you doing coming here dressed like that?' said a voice behind me. I turned round to see two big geezers in suits staring at me.

'You talking to me?' I replied, raising my voice above the DJ's 'I Feel Love'.

'Who else do you think I'm talking to?' replied the one with slicked-back hair. He then laughed and sneered, 'You're a scruffy-looking bugger.'

I ignored him, thinking to myself, 'I've got your card marked, mate.' No one talks to me like that and gets away with it. I then picked up my drinks and made my way across the crowded dance floor to the table in the corner where Jaffa, Joe, Ian and John were sitting. Looking around, I noticed that the big bloke was with a dozen other geezers at a table on the far side. They were all watching us.

'What's up?' asked John, seeing how angry I looked.

'See that geezer over there?' I said with a nod in the direction towards the far side of the club. 'I'm going to do him. He just called me a scruffy bugger.'

'Yeah, Al. You know what? It's the same lot that were taking the piss out of me earlier,' chimed Joe.

I was wearing a chunky white jumper, Levi jeans and tan Dealer boots, because I'd been working as a plasterer at an old people's home. After work, instead of going home to change, I'd met up with Jaffa, John and Joe at the George pub in Wanstead – Joe had just come out of prison that day. Ian joined us for a drink and then we all caught a mini-cab to the Room at the Top. Despite not being dressed for it, we knew that Big Terry, one of the bouncers there, would let us in.

'Well, let's have them, bruv,' said Jaffa eagerly.

'Okay, we'll do them after the club closes,' I said, still fuming at the attitude of the suit at the bar. 'John, take a glass down with you when you go, mate.'

The fact that there were only five of us and a dozen or so of them didn't bother us. We'd all had lots of tear-ups, and always enjoyed them. Joe – who once pulled a knife on me at Theydon Bois station after an argument following a big drinking session – was an out and out thug. I didn't know Ian, a skinny guy, that well.

As we planned what we'd do, Big Terry, sensing that something was wrong, came over to me. 'What's happening, Al?' he said, leaning across the table.

'Nothing to worry about,' I replied casually, lighting a fag.

'Remember. No trouble in here,' he warned.

'There won't be. Trust me. We're going to do them outside.'

Satisfied, he nodded and walked away.

At around midnight, the lights went on, the bar staff came out to collect the glasses, and people reluctantly started to make their way to the cloakroom and the lift, which was the only way in and out of the club, apart from the fire escape. This meant that things got a bit congested around the entrance when it came to closing time.

'Right, lads, you ready?' I said, downing my drink. They all nodded, stood up, and drained their glasses. But as we began to make our way to the lift, one of the bouncers told us to wait until the other firm had gone down first.

'Come on, man,' I pleaded.

'No. Hang on a bit,' he said firmly, holding up the palms of his hands.

After a few minutes Joe, Jaffa and John were ushered into the lift, but Ian and I had to wait as it was full. When we eventually got into the lift one of the doormen took us down and then back up again. He said that the lift wasn't working properly, but I knew he was trying to create some space between us and the other blokes. By now, I was raring to go.

When we came out of the building and into the cold night air, the other firm were standing across the road, taunting Jaffa, Joe and John, who was clutching a glass.

Even though it was gone midnight, the High Road was very busy with traffic, and people were waiting at bus stops, coming out of take-aways, milling around chatting, or looking for a mini-cab.

'Come on then!' screamed one of the geezers from across the road. 'What you waiting for?'

My adrenaline was pumping fast. I was going to teach these guys a lesson.

'Right!' yelled Jaffa. 'Let's go!'

The other blokes turned and ran off down the road, shouting back at us, and then disappeared into a side street. My heart was pounding as we chased after them. They were going to get a good hiding, one that they'd remember for a long time. We rounded the corner to find them standing in the middle of the street, with their arms outstretched.

That was it. I just steamed in and began lashing out with karate kicks. I got the big bloke up against the door of a blue Triumph Spitfire and began kicking him savagely in the face. My leg was going like a piston. By now everyone else had joined in. I can remember bottles and bricks flying through the air and seeing John tumble into a garden, and then whacking a geezer with a dustbin lid, and Jaffa falling into bushes with two others.

Suddenly, the big bloke caught me with a hook and I went down on the floor. As I got up, I grabbed a large piece of glass from a broken bottle and, holding it like a dagger, went at him. In a single movement, I slashed him down the face and then tried to stab him in his side. The next thing I was aware of was a searing pain through my hand. What was that?

Then I heard police sirens in the distance. Everyone stopped fighting, stood for a moment in the middle of the road, and then suddenly scattered in different directions. Myself and Ian legged it around the corner back into the High Road and then fled down the stairs into the underground car park beneath Harrison's and Gibson's. The door at the bottom wouldn't open, so I pushed it hard with my open hand. As I did, blood sprayed everywhere. I looked down and saw to my horror that one of my fingers was hanging off. Without thinking, I took my jumper off and wrapped it around my hand.

'Ian!'

'What?'

'I've got to get to hospital, mate,' I said. 'My finger's falling off.'

Ian and I left the car park by the rear exit and stood anxiously in the road waiting for a cab. Eventually one appeared and we flagged it down and told the driver to take us to King George's Hospital at Newbury Park. When we walked into Casualty, I told the nurse my name was Adam Ronson, the surname of the lead guitarist with the Spiders from Mars, and gave a moody (false) address. All I wanted to do was get the finger sewn up and go home.

Another nurse took me into a cubicle and told me to lie down on the bed and wait for a doctor. A few minutes later, Ian stuck his head around the cubicle curtain. He was visibly shaking. ''Ere, Al, that other firm's just walked in and that geezer you cut is in the next cubicle, and he's got a great big hole in his face. You can see right into his mouth.'

I hadn't expected this. 'Listen,' I told Ian, 'you'd better get gone, mate.'

'Okay. See you tomorrow.'

I looked at the various medical instruments on the table and thought, well, if they come for me, I'll stab them with a scalpel. And sure enough, the next moment one of the other firm appeared at the end of my bed, glaring at me. I reached for the scalpel and glared back at him. As I did this, a doctor walked in.

'What's going on?' he demanded, and then ordered the other geezer out of the cubicle.

The doctor examined my right hand and told me that it would have to be operated on. I didn't mind this as it would mean that I'd be kept in hospital and avoid the possibility of being attacked by the other firm.

A nurse then helped me into a wheelchair to be taken to a ward. But this meant that I had to go through Casualty, so I closed one eye and pretended to be half-unconscious as I was wheeled through. I can still remember the faces of the other firm, some of whom were with their girlfriends. They were itching to have a go at me, but the place was overrun with Old Bill.

The next morning, I woke up in a ward and found two Old Bill waiting at the end of the bed. 'We'd like to ask you a few questions,' said one of them.

'Ugh,' I answered, rolling over on my side. I figured that I needed to play for time in order to come up with a credible story. I'd no idea how seriously I'd hurt that bloke.

'Can you hear me?' repeated one of the Old Bill.

I ignored him and pretended to fall asleep. I then heard the Old Bill walk away, but I knew they'd be back. When I was sure they'd gone, I called one of the nurses over and gave her my real name and address, explaining that I'd given a moody name and address because my dad worked in the hospital and I didn't want him to know that I was injured. The real reason I did this, though, was that a false name might make it look as if I was guilty of something.

A doctor came to the side of my bed and told me that my finger would have to be amputated. I didn't like the thought of this and asked him if there were any other options. He replied that I could either have a tendon graft, which would mean staying in hospital for a couple of weeks, or have a piece of wire inserted in my hand to act as a tendon. I decided to go for the wire.

On Thursday afternoon, they operated on me. A thin piece of wire was put through to join the severed tendon and my arm was put in plaster. The following morning, I phoned my dad, who was in charge of stores at the hospital, and asked him if he'd take me home.

'Where are you?'

'On one of the wards.'

'One of the wards! What are you doing there?'

'Listen, it's a long story, Dad. I'm discharging myself. Can you meet me with the motor in the front of the hospital?'

My dad came to pick me up straightaway and I left, still wearing the hospital pyjamas, dressing gown and slippers. When I got home, Laura, my wife, was going out of her mind with worry. After I'd calmed her down and explained what had happened, she shook her head and said, 'Al, you've done it now. This sounds serious.'

'It'll be okay, love,' I said. But as soon as I said the words, I didn't really believe them. Something told me it wouldn't be okay.

I then went to The George in Wanstead to see if any of my firm were there, and to find out what had happened after I'd gone to hospital. I found Ian sitting at the bar, and he told me that Jaffa, John and Joe had been nicked.

That evening I sat in the living room chain-smoking and watching TV, as I tried to take my mind off what had happened. But I was worried. The Old Bill knew who I was and where I lived, and at 11 p.m. the inevitable happened. There was a knock at the door, and I opened it to find two serious-looking blokes in suits standing there. I knew instantly that they were CID.

'Alan Mortlock?' asked the older one in a stern voice.

'Yeah,' I replied, thinking that there was no point in lying.

'I'm arresting you in connection with an incident near the Room at the Top night club. You're coming with us to Ilford nick.'

I nodded resignedly. Laura appeared behind me. 'What's happening, Al?'

'Nothing to worry about, love,' I said, turning to her. 'I've just got to go to the nick to answer a few questions. Don't worry.' I grabbed my coat and then followed the two plods to the unmarked Old Bill car parked outside. As I got into the back, I thought to myself, I'm in it big time now.

# 2

# The Rebel

When I was eight, my Uncle Joe, who used to box in the Royal Navy, bought me my first pair of boxing gloves. They were brown leather with horse hair inside, and had long laces and a musty smell. They seemed massive, and my hands felt lost inside when I put them on. Standing in the living room, he'd show me how to jab, punch, duck and do the old one-two.

There was a strong tradition of boxing in my family. My dad boxed in the RAF, and I can remember him telling me how he used to win coupons, which he'd spend in the NAFI, or buy glass bowls, which he gave to his mum. And my Uncle Dick was the Army middleweight champion of the Empire.

I used to watch the boxing when it came on the TV. I particularly remember Cassius Clay, later Mohammad Ali, fighting Henry Cooper. But I preferred watching wrestling. I thought people like Mick McManus, Jackie Pallo, Adrian Street and Kendo Nagasaki were fantastic. My dad and I used to wrestle in the living room – he was pretty rough.

I'm an East Ender and proud of it. I was born on 12 October 1955 at 1 Eve Road, Plaistow. My dad, who was one of eleven children, was also from the East End, Stratford. He was a real grafter and did a variety of jobs. He worked as a roofer, chauffeur, tobacconist, transport manager and also laid tennis courts.

My mum was born in Belfast, but she moved to England and grew up in Eltham, south-east London. Her dad was the footballer Billy Gillespie, who played for both Sheffield United and Northern Ireland. She had ten sisters and a brother. Like Dad, she did lots of different jobs over the years – she worked as a beauty consultant for Helena Rubinstein, was a barmaid, and managed the Wimpy Bar in High Road, Leytonstone.

Dad and Mum first met when they both worked at Briggs Motor Bodies, a subsidiary of Ford's, in Dagenham. My mum was very attractive and had auburn hair. Looking at the photos of her from those days, she looked a little bit like the actress Joan Crawford.

When I was two my dad bought a newsagent's and tobacconist's shop at Maryland Point in Stratford, near Maryland Station, and we moved into the flat above. Across the road was Taplow's brewery, which had an advertisement for Sandemans Port above the main entrance. Early each morning the brewery workers would come into the shop for their newspapers and tobacco.

I can remember staring wide-eyed at the barley twists, sherbet lemons, wine gums and long sticks of aniseed in the jars on the shelves. And I used to love the triangular-shaped Jubbly ice lollies and also the Wall's Heart ice lollies, which were shaped like hearts. My dad also used to sell toys, and I remember once pestering him for a Zorro pop gun, which he eventually gave me.

My first school was Davies Lane Infants School. I hated it at first and just wanted to stay at home, but eventually I settled in. When I was six we moved to a semi-detached corner house in Landsdowne Road, Leytonstone. From my bedroom window I could see the trains which ran along the railway line above.

After me, my mum didn't have any more children. She had three miscarriages, two before I was born, and one after. Some only children are very lonely when they are growing up, but I wasn't. We used to have some great family parties when all my uncles, aunties and cousins would get together for a knees-up.

I remember playing in the summer with my mates on Wanstead Flats, a large green area made up of trees, scrubland, football pitches and a pond. A lot of the boys I played with were a few years older than me. Back then, there were still a few bomb sites around, and they were a bit like a treasure trove. You could find all sorts of things there, such as old toys, coins, jewellery and tins.

My mum was an alcoholic. I think her heavy drinking had started well before she met Dad. When he went out to work she'd start drinking from bottles she'd hidden somewhere in the house. Her favourite drink was VP Wine, a cross between a wine and a sherry.

When Dad was working nights she'd usually slip out to the pub, taking me with her. In those days, children weren't allowed in pubs, so I'd have to wait outside. I must have spent hours and hours standing outside some pub or other. I remember standing in the freezing cold in the alley that ran down the side of The Crown in High Road, Leytonstone, one Christmas, and staring longingly at the toys in Bearman's department store across the road and wondering why I wasn't at home in the warm.

One image that has stayed with me from those times is that of a big brass handle on the door of The Crown pub. When someone opened it, I'd see my mum sitting on a stool at the bar, laughing and joking with her friends. Sometimes she'd send me out a glass of lemonade and some biscuits.

On occasions, she would take me to one of her mate's houses to wait for her. I didn't like them, and they didn't like me. And I didn't want to be there, and they didn't want me there.

Sometimes when I was out with her she'd go into a ladies' toilet to drink or she'd do it on a park bench. I didn't like it at all and knew that it wasn't right. I used to see her face change – she started to look ugly and sad when she started drinking heavily.

Dad also liked a drink, but he was what you'd call a social drinker. 'Everything in moderation' was my dad's motto, and he used to say, 'When the drink is in; the wits are out.' He smoked Old Holborn and Golden Virginia, which had a great smell. Sitting at the table,

I'd cut up the tobacco for him on a copy of the *Evening News* and then scoop it into one of his tins.

Mum and Dad used to row and fight a lot, but my dad put up with bundles of aggravation. I can remember once when I was nine, and my mum was sitting in the chair playing 'Silence is Golden', by the Tremeloes, over and over again. When my dad came in from work, he asked her to put something else on. 'Put a happy song on,' he said, 'something like "Any Old Iron".' She refused, and then they had another blazing row.

There were times when my mum became violent and would attack my dad. She'd pick anything up, a knife, a bottle, a vase, but he never hit her back. Instead, he'd try and hold her down, wrestle her to the ground, or just walk out of the house.

I hated the rows and violence and just wanted it to stop. Sometimes I'd put myself between them in an attempt to separate them. What all of this did was to instil fear into me. I was always frightened that they were going to start rowing or fighting, or that one of them would walk out and not come back.

Finally, this happened. My dad left home for a year and lived with one of his sisters. He was working as a baker at this point and had to be up at 4 a.m., but Mum was coming in at all hours and he wasn't getting much sleep. I think he did it to make a point to her. He was saying that if she didn't stop drinking, he'd leave her for good. He'd had enough.

After he had left was one of the lowest points in my life. When he used to come to see me on Saturdays, I never wanted him to go. This was because after he'd gone, my mum would take me to the pub with her or start boozing in the house. During this time, she would also bring a lot of strangers back home. They used to scare me; I hated it and couldn't wait for them to leave. Yet I didn't blame either my mum or dad; I blamed alcohol.

But there were also some very happy times amid all this darkness. On Saturdays I'd get my pocket money, and I'd spend most of it on Airfix soldiers and civil war cards. We'd usually go shopping in the afternoon to one of the local markets – Romford, East Ham or

Queens Road – where my mum would always buy traditional East End food, such as cockles and mussels, pease puddings and faggots. Sometimes we'd buy jellied eels from Tubby Isaac's stall in Petticoat Lane Market. And we would always go into a pub for an hour or two.

Holidays usually meant a few days in Great Yarmouth or days out to Southend, where I'd spend most of my pocket money in the shooting gallery. I remember once smashing a kid's bike up and my dad having to pay for it out of the money he'd saved up to take us on holiday to Cornwall.

On one trip to Southend, when I was ten, we were at the Kursall Amusement Park. Suddenly, my mum pulled a face and propped herself up against a wall.

'What's up, Mum?' I asked, worried.

'I've got double vision, love,' she replied, squinting her eyes.

Later that week, she went to see her GP and he sent her to hospital for tests, but the doctors couldn't diagnose what the problem was.

My mum and dad also held seances in the house, and various members of the family would come along. They'd sit around the table and someone would write the letters of the alphabet on cards and put them in a circle. Another set of cards, numbered one to ten, and two with 'yes' and 'no' written on them, would be placed around a glass in the middle. Someone would then put a finger on the glass and call on a guardian spirit for a dead member of the family. The glass would then move to different letters and form a message, which someone else would write down. I used to find it very scary, and I always remember that there was a strange, eerie feeling on the landing – and I often felt frightened at night in my bedroom. I didn't know why this was.

When I was eleven we moved to Highfield Road, Woodford Bridge, an area built around St Paul's church, a village green, and an old pub called The Crown and Crooked Billet. At the end of Highfield Road was a large sports ground which you could walk through to reach the River Rodin.

Situated on the border of east London and Essex, Woodford Bridge wasn't as built up as Leytonstone. Instead of narrow streets of small terraced houses, it contained more imposing-looking houses, largely occupied by families from the East End who'd done well for themselves and had decided to leave working-class areas such as Leytonstone, Stepney, Canning Town and Bethnal Green for the more leafy fringes of London. To the north of Woodford Bridge were the more affluent areas of Chigwell and Loughton. It was a case of the more money you had, the farther away from the East End you moved.

My mum's double vision gradually got worse, and despite tests at various hospitals, the doctors were unable to find out what the problem was. I remember when she was kept in the London Hospital in Whitechapel Road, I used to nip across the road to a deli to buy her salt beef sandwiches, which she loved. Eventually, it was discovered that she had an aneurysm, a ballooning of the main artery to the brain, and she underwent a major operation.

Having failed my eleven-plus at Davies Lane Junior School, I was sent to St Barnabas Boys School in St Barnabas Road, Woodford Green. I'd left all my friends behind in Leytonstone, and at first found it difficult to make new friends, feeling that I was an outsider.

I hated going to St Barnabas and was always playing truant. The deputy headmaster, Mr White, who was nicknamed Squeaker, because his shoes used to squeak when he walked down the corridor, visited my house regularly to take me back to school. I'd often run out of the house when he arrived. I started to become more and more aggressive and to care even less about my studies, and before long I got to be friends with the hard guys in the school.

Early one morning, a prefect stopped me in the corridor and asked me where I was going. I replied that it was none of his business. When he persisted in questioning me, I head-butted him. At the assembly, my name was read out and I was told to report to Mr Squeaker's office afterwards. I did, but when he told me to bend over because he was going to cane me, I refused and walked out.

I began nicking from shops when I was about twelve. On the way to the Saturday morning pictures at the Majestic in High Road, Woodford, my mates and I would go into Woolworth's and take stuff such as chocolates, sweets, toys and Parker pens.

The first alcoholic drink I ever had was one warm, summer evening when I was thirteen. My mum and dad took me and my mate Chris to The Black Deer in Debden, Essex, which was run by Freddy Cooper, a relation and a former West Ham United player. Chris and I sat on the wall outside and my dad brought bottles of brown ale out to us. When I got home I was as sick as a dog.

By the time I reached fourteen I was drinking regularly, usually Ind Coope Light Ale. I managed to get served in all the pubs in the area because I looked older than my age. I think the tattoos helped in this. When I came home at night I'd often walk around the streets for an hour to sober up. My dad knew I was drinking, I think, but he never said anything.

In my third year at school I became a skinhead. I first became aware of skinheads when I went to the fun-fair at Wanstead Flats, and I noticed all these guys with cropped hair, wearing boots and three-quarter length trousers with braces. I thought they looked great and immediately wanted to be one of them. I didn't adopt the skinhead look straightaway, but gradually – over the next few weeks – I bought a pair of brown Doc Martens, started wearing Brutus and Ben Sherman shirts, and rolled-up trousers that had braces. My hair was quite short anyway, but eventually I had it cropped.

Being a skinhead gave me a sense of belonging and an identity. In our Woodford Bridge crew were John Hawkins, Martin Brindley, Mickey Page, Charlie Webb, Dave Nixon, Jack Sainty, Dave Wartnarby and a few others. I was nicknamed Mort. We also had a number of skinhead girls who hung around with us.

I used to meet with the crew by the bronze statue of Winston Churchill on the green alongside The Castle pub in Woodford Green. Sometimes as many as fifty of us would turn up. If there weren't any rockers or bikers to have a tear-up with, we'd fight other skinheads from places such as Mile End, Debden, Loughton, Walthamstow and Ilford. If you were walking down the road and you met another crew of skinheads, they'd often shout out, 'Who are you screwing?' This meant 'What are you looking at?' And the next minute it would kick off.

All my mates had tattoos, and when I was thirteen I had 'Mum and Dad' tattooed on my arm by Ben Gunn at his house in Old Church Road, Chingford. Ben was covered from head to foot in tattoos. Every time he did a tattoo he'd shake his head and say, 'Must be mad. Marked for life.' My mum didn't like me doing this, and when I went to have two more tattoos done, she phoned Ben and told him that if he tattooed me again she'd report him to the Old Bill. So I went to another tattooist, in Romford, who was nicknamed 'the butcher', and he did my second tattoo. But he made a terrible job of it.

Also about this time, my dad bought me a metallic blue and orange Vespa SS180 scooter with chrome side panels. Some of my mates also had Vespas, and we'd often ride to North Woolwich and catch the ferry across the river to Jack Ringo's tattoo shop in Woolwich. We all loved going there – on the walls were frayed sheets of paper showing hundreds of tattoo designs, and there was a pinball machine and a juke box in one corner.

Six of us went there one day but, finding it closed, we went to The Woolwich Infant pub to wait for Jack to come back. When we returned to the shop an hour later, it was open, and we trooped in to find a greaser, a scruffy guy with long hair and wearing a leather jacket, sitting in the chair and having a tattoo done on his arm. We took our seats and waited our turn. Soon the shop began to fill up with more greasers, Hell's Angels and a few teddy boys. There was an uneasy feeling as we all sat there or stood around, glancing at each other. It's going to go off any minute, I thought to myself.

And I was right. After we'd had our tattoos done, we went outside and got on our scooters. As we did so, some greasers came at us and started kicking and punching us. We fought back, but as we were well outnumbered we figured our best bet was to jump on our scooters and head back to the ferry. So we sped away, leaving the greasers swearing and shouting at us in the road.

Two of my friends were members of Garden City Amateur Boxing Club juniors in Woodford Bridge, and one evening I thought I'd go and see what it was like. The club was situated in a complex of big, old buildings that housed orphans, and was known locally as Dr Barnardo's village. The first thing that I noticed when I walked into the gym was that the posts of the ring were set in triangles of concrete. I remember thinking to myself, if your head hits that concrete, you're in trouble. There were about twenty boys there. The instructor told us all to take a skipping rope and warm up. As I'd never skipped in my life, I found it very difficult. He then told us all to take a pair of gloves off a long table and start hitting the punch bags. After ten minutes or so of this, he called out my name and told me to get into the ring.

Surprised, I squeezed under the ropes and stood in the middle of the ring. The next thing, Steven Sloane, a senior who'd had lots of amateur fights, came bouncing into the ring. He was about three years older than me and had a boxer's nose. I was just dressed in a T-shirt and jeans, but he was wearing a gown, and boxing shorts and boots. His dad then got into the ring and said that he was going to referee the fight. Looking at Steven, who was huffing and puffing and dancing around, I thought he looked like a proper boxer, and I felt a bit nervous. His father gave us the signal to begin. I faced Steven, taking up a position my Uncle Joe had taught me. Bang! Bang! Bang! He began to hit me all around the ring. I tried my best to land some punches, but he parried each one and then hit me again. Bang! I'd thought that boxing gloves would prevent the punches hurting me; but it was just the opposite – but he never managed to knock me down.

Afterwards, I felt very angry that I'd just been used as cannon fodder for Steven Sloane, and I never went back to Garden City. Soon after, with my mate John Hawkins, I joined the Wado Ru karate club in Theydon Bois in Essex. At the time, I used to watch all the kung fu films on TV and the Chinese martial arts films at the Plaza cinema in South Woodford. I immediately took to karate, and reckoned I could become good at it.

To get some money, I started a Saturday job at the Co-op in Snakes Lane, Woodford, where I did everything from shelf stacking to unloading vans. When I swept the floor at the end of the day, I used to go behind the cash tills and knock packets of Players Number 6 fags and Golden Virginia tobacco on to the floor and then shovel them into the rubbish bag, take it outside, remove the fags, and throw them over the wall – where my mum would be waiting on the other side. She thought it was a good laugh.

By now, I was a rebel at school. I was constantly getting into fights and disrupting lessons, and I'd been banned from school outings. 'Who do you think you are? The Kray Twins?' Mr Affleck, the headmaster, once asked me and my mate Leon after he had called us into his office to cane us. Art and sport were the only subjects I liked. At fourteen, I became the 400-metre school champion and I also ran for Essex.

My school years came to an abrupt end after an incident at the school sports day. My mum turned up to watch me run, but I could tell from the way she spoke that she'd been drinking beforehand. She got into an argument with a man – another parent. When I saw him pulling her arm, I ran over and hit him across the face with my mum's umbrella. A teacher then got involved, and I whacked him too. The Old Bill were called and Mum and I were put in the back of a Morris Minor panda car and taken to Woodford Green nick. But we weren't charged. Later that evening my dad came in his car to get us; he wasn't pleased with what had happened, and there was a stony silence between him and Mum on the journey home.

The next morning, instead of wearing my school uniform I put on a pair of rolled-up Levi jeans, a gingham shirt, braces, and Doc Marten boots. As I swaggered through the gates, I knew I was going to get expelled, but this was what I wanted. Mr Affleck saw me and called me into his office.

'What do you mean by turning up to school dressed like that? Take those braces off,' he ordered.

I laughed at him. 'You what?'

'Bend over,' he said, picking up his cane.

'You ain't using that on me.'

'Mortlock, I'm expelling you,' he said sternly.

'I ain't bothered,' I shrugged, and walked out. That was the end of my education, and I had no regrets.

I was too young to work full time, so I hung around with my mates, and we'd go out with girls and nick from shops. Sometimes we'd go into a church and sit at the back during a service. To annoy the vicar, my mate Dave Wartnarby would often burp out loud.

My first full-time job was as a sales assistant at Burtons in Loughton High Street, but I only lasted a week, as I found it boring. What's more, they never even supplied me with a suit – and it was impossible to nick one. I had to buy one from another shop, because I couldn't afford Burtons prices.

My next job – working on the lorries unloading and loading boxes of fruit from Covent Garden Fruit and Vegetable Market – was even worse. I lasted one night. I can still remember the smell of oranges and bananas and the shouting and whistling of the blokes working there.

I then got a job at Quill's greengrocer's in George Lane, South Woodford. But I hated being cooped up inside, and after a few months I left and got a job as a labourer with a building company in Wanstead. The work was hard, but it was more up my street. The owner, Mr Chuck, drove a red metallic Bentley, and his son, a real flash guy, had a white Porsche. Mr Chuck was a portly figure, who looked like a cross between Robert Maxwell and Denis Healey.

And it was during this time that I met a girl called Laura, who was to become my wife. She was fourteen and still at school. I was working on a building site in Woodford Green and I used to see her going to a fish and chip shop next door. I was attracted to her immediately because she had long brown-blonde hair and a great figure. I think that she liked my Jack-the-lad image, and knew that I'd been out with nearly all of her mates.

She began offering me chips, and I'd show off by jumping twenty-five feet off the scaffold and land in the sand below. After standing her up a few times, we started going out regularly, although from time to time we broke up. Laura was a lot quieter than me, but she loved coming out on the back of my scooter and going dancing. I remember that she had posters of David Cassidy, the Beatles and David Bowie on her bedroom wall. Like me, she was an only child.

Her parents were Jewish and they lived in a big house in Woodford Green. Her dad ran Marks of the Lane delicatessen on the corner of Wentworth Street and Middlesex Street (known as Petticoat Lane). It was well known for its smoked salmon bagels and salt beef sandwiches.

But Laura's parents didn't like me at all: they thought I wasn't good enough for her. Sometimes her dad used to lock her in her room, so that she wasn't able to meet me. One evening, he turned up in The White Hart. I think he was going to have a go at me, but, seeing that I was with all my mates, he didn't. I bought him a drink and tried to let him see that I wasn't as bad as he thought.

After about six months I left the building company and did a succession of jobs, including working at Dalston Plating and Hedin Heat, an electrical parts company, both of which were on the Raven Road Factory Estate in Woodford Green.

One day, Mum and I went to Ilford to do some shopping, and on the way back she got off the bus at the stop near our house, while I stayed on to go and see Laura. She wasn't in, so I walked back home. As I turned into Highfield Road, I saw one of my mates running towards me.

'Al! Al!' he shouted. 'Your house has burnt down.'

'You what?' I replied, thinking he was taking the mickey. 'What are you on about?'

'No, it's true.'

Peering ahead, I could see a cloud of smoke. As I neared the house, I stopped dead in shock. Fire engines blocked the road and there just seemed to be a smouldering shell where my house had been. All I could think about were my pairs of Levi stay-press trousers and Brutus shirts, which I'd bought from Granditers clothes shop in High Road, Ilford.

My mum and dad were devastated. It turned out that the fire had been started by a faulty electrical heater. We spent that night in a hotel and then went to live in a housing association cottage in Grove End, nearby. When the insurance money came through, my dad refurbished the house in Highfield Road and we moved back. He also gave me money to replace my trousers and shirts.

But a far worse tragedy was to come. One night, I was woken up by a terrible moaning sound coming from my mum's room. Alarmed, I leapt out of bed and ran to find out what was the matter.

'What's up, Mum?'

'My arms and legs feel dead,' she replied, screwing up her eyes in agony. Earlier in the evening she'd complained of a terrible headache.

I started to gently rub her arms and legs. My dad, who had been in a deep sleep, then woke up. I told him everything was OK and to go back to sleep. After a while, Mum told me to go back to bed. About half an hour later I heard her moaning again, only this time it was even worse. So I ran back in and woke my dad up, and told him to phone for an ambulance. By this time, Mum seemed to be semi-conscious. I put my head on her chest and listened to her heart, but it didn't seem to be beating. I started pumping her heart like they did on the TV programme *Police Surgeon*.

For the very first time in my life, I prayed. 'Please, God, don't let my mum die!' I said.

Her heart started to beat very quickly. I then gave her the kiss of life, but she suddenly went motionless. I held up a mirror to her breath to see if she was still breathing, but there was nothing. A sense of numbness overcame me.

It took the ambulance ages to arrive. When it did, I went ballistic at the ambulance men when they told me that they'd gone to the wrong address. Only my dad prevented me from hitting one of them with a chair. I was so angry that my dad had to lock me in the bathroom to calm me down. When he finally let me out, I remember seeing the ambulance men wheeling my mum through the front door. Her head was lolled to one side. Somehow, I knew she was dead.

Dad and I both travelled in the back of the ambulance with her to Whipps Cross Hospital. All I could think about during the journey was that I wanted to do the man who had taken the call on the switchboard. When we reached the hospital, I was raging, and demanded to be taken to the switchboard office. One of the ambulance men told me that the call wasn't taken at the hospital, but at a central switchboard.

At this point, a young doctor came over and tried to calm me down. 'Did your mum like dancing?' he asked gently.

'Yeah. Why?' I replied, puzzled. What was he asking such a stupid question for?

'Well, if she'd have lived, she would have been a vegetable. She had a massive stroke and a brain haemorrhage. She would have been paralysed and wouldn't have been able to walk or feed herself.' He paused. 'Would you have wanted your mother to be like that? Would your mum have wanted that?'

I shook my head. 'No.'

When I got back home, at about 4 a.m., I fell asleep in front of the gas fire in the front room like I used to do when I was younger. When I woke up in the morning I looked around for Mum. I thought it strange that the curtains were drawn and the lights were on. Dad was sitting in a chair at the far end of the living room, writing at the table. Then it hit me. Mum was dead. It was a terrible feeling. Not knowing what to do, I went out and spent an hour in a haze just wandering round the streets, trying to take it all in.

Later that afternoon, I went with my dad and Auntie Nell to visit my mum in the chapel of rest at the funeral home in George Lane, and what really struck me was her face. I will never forget her angry expression. It said, 'I don't want to die!' Auntie Nell remarked that my mum would never go anywhere without her make-up on, so I went to a chemist's across the road and bought some lipstick and eye shadow. I went back to the funeral home and tried to apply the make-up to my mum's face, but it wouldn't adhere properly, so I asked the funeral director to do it.

On the day of the funeral, at the City of London Crematorium, in Aldersbrook Road, Manor Park, I broke down. I was fifteen. Sitting in the chapel, with all my family around me, I just felt that I wanted to be on my own. During the short service I felt a despair start to well up inside of me and I fought to hold back the tears. As the coffin disappeared into the cremator, I heard myself sobbing uncontrollably. My dad put his arm around me.

Looking out of the window of the funeral car as we drove back to the house for the reception, I spotted an ex-girlfriend strolling along Chigwell Road, and I thought to myself that none of this seemed real.

The following week, I went to Ben Gunn's and had a tattoo done on my arm. It said, 'In Memory of Mum'.

In the days and weeks that followed, neither Dad nor I could really come to terms with the death of Mum, and it was a couple of months later that he took me to a Spiritualist church in Washington Road, South Woodford.

'Don't tell anyone anything about yourself,' he warned, as we walked into the small church.

'Okay, Dad.'

Halfway through the service the medium, a small, elderly woman, who was standing on the stage, said, 'Is there anybody there with the letter A?'

Remembering what my dad had told me, I said nothing.

'Is there someone by the name of Alan here?' she asked, looking around. 'I have a woman in front of me with bright red hair and a lovely bunch of flowers. She's about five foot one and she says she wants to speak to Alan.'

This is my mum she's talking about, I thought to myself. But how does this old woman know about her? What's more, when the medium had approached the stage, a couple of people had had to help her up because she was so frail. But now she seemed to have the movements of a much younger woman.

'She says that you made the right choice with the trousers you bought. And she says you must learn a trade,' she continued.

I was amazed. The week before I'd gone with Auntie Nell to the market to buy some trousers. Unable to make up my mind which ones to buy, I'd asked for her opinion. And my mum had always encouraged me to take up a trade.

Holding her head, the medium suddenly screamed out, 'There's a terrible pain! A terrible pain!'

I was stunned, and felt that this was the pain my mum had experienced when she'd had the stroke and brain haemorrhage. I wanted to burst out crying, but somehow I held back the tears.

As we left the church, my dad said to me, 'It was right what she said.'

'Yeah,' I nodded. I felt happier because of what the medium had said, but by the time I got home this feeling had been replaced by anger. Thinking of my mum's death, I felt that I'd been robbed of something important and that my life would never be the same again.

# 3

# Tough Guy

East London is known as a tough area, and this goes back to the time when the docks were in full swing. In those days, thieving, drinking and violence were common in the streets and pubs. For example, one of my uncles got into a row with another docker and ended up having his eye gouged out with a hook. I knew that to gain respect in east London, you had to establish a reputation, and you did this by having a tear-up.

By this time I was regularly getting into tear-ups, for one reason or another. When I was about sixteen I let my cropped hair grow out and started wearing sheepskin coats and Italian box-weave shoes. Those of us who dressed in this way were often called suede heads because of our hairstyles.

The White Hart in Woodford Bridge, which was situated on Chigwell Road, at the top of a hill near the green, became my local. It was a big Victorian pub with a horseshoe public bar and a saloon bar, where they held discos at the weekend. One evening I was in there with Mickey Page, Charlie Webb and some other mates when through the window I saw about twenty greasers on motorbikes pull into the car park. They came into the pub, ordered their drinks, and started looking over at the table where we were sitting and leering at us. Even though they were older than me, and most of them were bigger, I wasn't worried. I was out to prove myself. I glared back.

'Shall we do 'em?' I said to my mates. They all nodded enthusiastically. 'Well, let's wait until they leave. We'll have them in the car park.'

After about half an hour, the greasers trooped out of the pub, jeering at us. We immediately got up and followed them into the car park. I then kicked one of their motorbikes over.

'Oi! What you doing?' shouted a greaser, running towards me.

I lashed out at him and caught him bang on the chin, and what followed next was like something out of a western. It went off big time. Noticing a crash helmet spinning on the floor, I picked it up and whacked a geezer with it. I saw Charlie laying into two other greasers. Realising that they were beaten, the greasers quickly mounted their bikes and roared away.

When a fight starts in a pub, I often hear a distinctive rumbling sound, a bit like a stampede or an Underground train coming out of the tunnel, and I don't really see much around me. When it's over, and most fights don't last longer than a few minutes, it's a bit like coming up from swimming underwater. If you know it's about to go off, you feel a tension running through you.

In your mind you're trying to work out what you are going to do and what the other guy is likely to do. I could always tell if someone was about to have a row by reading their body language. If they stood confidently and looked me straight in the eye, then I could guarantee they weren't just being mouthy. It's crucial to get the first punch, head-butt or kick in. My natural instinct was to land a kick at the head, but this wasn't always a good idea, as you could lose your balance, especially if you'd had a drink.

A night club I used to go to was Oscar's at the Green Gate in Newbury Park. Despite her protestations, I'd sometimes leave Laura sitting on her own at a table and then wait at the bar until some guy came over to chat her up. When he did, I'd walk over, ask him what he was doing, and then head-butt him.

I never worried about the bouncers in clubs. One of the bouncers at Oscar's was called Karate Mick, who was about six foot six, and had a blond droopy moustache and a square haircut. We never spoke, but we both knew that each other did martial arts, so there was a mutual respect there.

The guv'nor was well known for taking people out of the side door and giving them a kicking. One night, I was standing alone at the bar, and the guv'nor and some of the bouncers were standing chatting next to me. I went to pick up my pint glass and then accidentally dropped it.

'Sorry, mate,' I said apologetically.

The guv'nor turned to me with a menacing look. 'You know where you're going?'

'Where?'

'Out the side door.'

Oh no, I'm not, I thought, and I head-butted him as hard as I could. He fell back against the bar, sending an ash-tray crashing to the floor. Before the doormen could do anything, I started running towards the exit. I felt like the Six Million Dollar Man, as if I were running in slow motion. As I reached the exit I saw Karate Mick blocking it. Here we go, I thought. But he just stepped aside, opened the door, and let me out.

The next day, I went to see a mate who lived around the corner from Karate Mick. As I walked down the street, I saw Karate Mick washing his Lincoln Continental car. He acknowledged me with a friendly nod.

'Thanks for last night,' I said.

'No problem,' he said quietly, putting down his bucket. 'I've never liked the guv'nor.'

'Well, cheers anyway, man.'

Looking back, I have wondered whether some of the violence I engaged in wasn't a result of the anger I felt at my mum's death. If I was at a disco and I heard Bill Withers singing 'Lean on Me', which was a favourite of my mum's, or the Four Tops singing 'Reach Out I'll Be There', I'd feel the emotions welling up inside of me and I'd nearly always start a fight.

John Hawkins, who I'd known since school, started hanging around with me a lot. He was a couple of years younger than me – a very loud, funny guy, who liked to sing dirty songs and chat up the birds. As we came out of Ilford Palais at about 1 a.m. one night, he decided to nick a car. We were both a bit drunk. John was potty about driving and his weakness was nicking cars. He used to enjoy just nicking them and then dumping them.

'See that green mini, Al, we'll take that,' he said, as we stood looking up and down the street.

'Yeah, okay, mate.' I figured it would be good fun.

He then got out the bunch of car keys he always carried with him and started trying them in the lock. Eventually, there was a click and the door opened. 'Right, in you get,' he said, as he eased himself behind the wheel and fiddled with the ignition.

I got in the passenger seat, and the next minute we were tearing off down the road, laughing out loud. Then he let me have a go behind the wheel, and I ended up driving down the pavement. Finally, we abandoned the car in a quiet side street and walked away, laughing.

'Let's nick that Ford Corsair outside the newsagents,' he said, hurrying across the road. 'Come on.'

He managed to open the door quite easily, and I jumped in and we sped away. Eventually we ended up somewhere in Barking. Looking around the dark street, neither of us were sure exactly where we were. Then I heard a siren and, in the wing mirror, I saw an Old Bill van coming down the road at speed.

'Old Bill, John!' I shouted.

Before he had time to do anything, the Old Bill van had pulled across the road, blocking our exit. Two Old Bill got out and walked towards us. One of them then rapped on the window.

'Right. Out you get,' he said, shining his flashlight at us. We got out and stood there, looking sheepish. 'Is this your car?' asked one of them.

'Yeah,' John mumbled.

'What's the registration number?'

'Er, can't remember,' he spluttered.

That was it. We were then put in the back of the Old Bill van and told that we were being taken to Barking nick. When I heard this, I was worried because Barking nick had a fearsome reputation for giving you a kicking. Just as some pubs get reputations for trouble, so do some nicks.

The cell door slammed shut, giving me a start. I sat on the bench and, looking at all the graffiti scrawled on the walls, wondered what had happened to all the people who had sat there before me. For a moment, I was overcome by a fear that I was never going to get out.

An hour or so later, I heard a cell door open and an Old Bill tell John that his dad had arrived to take him home. Shortly after, my cell door also swung open and I was taken by an Old Bill to a small room, where I was charged with taking and driving away a car and then, to my great relief, I was released. A few weeks later, John and I appeared at Barking Magistrates Court, where we were each fined ten quid and I had my scooter licence endorsed.

Like me, John loved a tear-up. But he nearly came a cropper one night. We were drinking in the Red House pub, opposite Redbridge tube station, when he got into an argument at the pool table with a guy, and the two of them went outside to sort it out. I followed them to the car park and stood there watching as they exchanged blows. John was winning to begin with, but then the other guy got him down on the floor and started pounding him.

'Al, get him off me!' he cried.

'No, John, you look like you're doing all right to me, mate,' I replied with a grin. I watched for a little longer and then decided John had had enough, so I kicked the guy off and he ran away down the road. Clutching his ear, John got up off the floor.

'What's up, mate?' I asked.

Looking at his hand, he said, 'He's bitten my ear!'

I started taking drugs when I was seventeen. There were two kinds, uppers and downers. Uppers, which were speed, would make you hyper, while downers, which were sleeping tablets, would make you feel very laid back. I used to buy ten of them for a quid from a guy called Rob. He used to buy them either from hippies or a dealer at The Red Lion in High Road, Leytonstone. He'd also get people to get their GP to prescribe certain drugs, such as antidepressants. Once they'd cashed in the prescription at the chemist, Rob would buy the drugs off them.

One Saturday afternoon, Rob came to my house. He went to the bathroom and returned with the mirror. Sitting down in the kitchen, he placed the mirror on the table and then pulled out a small white packet.

'What's that?' I asked, puzzled.

'It's speed,' he replied, taking out a knife from his pocket. He undid the packet, emptied the white powder on to the mirror, and began to chop it into lines with the knife. He then rolled a fiver into a tube, held it up to his nose, and inhaled the powder.

'Want to try some?'

'Okay.'

I took the tube from him and sniffed the powder. I immediately felt a sensation in the bridge of my nose, then I had a butterfly feeling in the pit of my stomach. After about twenty minutes, I had this terrific feeling. I felt incredibly happy, light and full of energy.

'This is the business, man,' I chuckled.

Card games and thieving used to provide me with extra money. I usually played three card brag. There were always card games in The Railway Tavern in Snakes Lane, Woodford, where a lot of the dustmen would go when they'd finished their work for the day, and also at The George in Eastern Avenue, Wanstead. When the pub closed at 3 p.m. I'd often carry on playing cards at a mate's house and then return to the pub when it reopened at 6 p.m.

I used to go into shops in an overcoat and leave with a suit underneath it. And I sometimes stole camera equipment to order for a bricklayer I worked for. This was just part of the culture I grew up in, although I never thought of robbing people's houses.

The thinking was that if you wanted to buy a new pair of jeans or shoes, then you'd try and nick them.

Despite my thieving, I always wanted to work, and I got a job in an iron foundry on the banks of the River Rodin, where I had to carry shanks of white-hot metal. It was a great atmosphere because a lot of my mates worked there. I had a row there one day with a guy who was winding me up, and I hit him with a metal lid from one of the pots.

When I was eighteen I met Phil Laing, a top martial arts expert and someone with a fierce reputation on the streets. 'You don't mess with Phil,' everyone used to say. He was about twenty-five, solid muscle and, with his jet black hair and five o'clock shadow, he reminded me of a pirate.

I once heard a story about the time Phil went to Woolston Hall, which later became Epping Forest Country Club, to look for work. He was challenged by this big bloke, who started effing and blinding at him. Phil kept his cool and told the bloke to calm down, explaining that he'd only come to see if there was any work available. But the bloke carried on and threatened to do Phil. Well, Phil decided he'd had enough and he set about him. When the police were called and they saw the state of the guy, Phil was arrested and charged with using a weapon. But he hadn't used a weapon – he'd only used his hands and legs. Eventually, all charges were dropped as it was decided that he had acted in self-defence.

I joined his Bushido kung fu classes at a church hall in Shernhall Street, Walthamstow. In Japanese 'Bushido' means the way of the warrior. This style of kung fu was known as full contact and it meant that you could kick, punch, knee, elbow, grapple, throw and use arm and wrist locks. It was a bit like karate, ju jitsu, Thai boxing and wrestling all rolled into one. I loved it.

We used to wear fingerless gloves, similar to those Bruce Lee wore in the film *Enter the Dragon*. At the time, the TV series *Kung Fu*, starring David Carradine, was being shown. In each episode you'd see the scene when he left the monastery and had to pick up a red-hot urn. I remember an instructor from another club once showing me two large burn marks that he'd got as a result of imitating David Carradine. But even this instructor refused to fight Phil. I became one of Phil's top students and we also became firm friends.

When necessary, I used the techniques I'd learned from Phil when I was out. For example, once when I was at a party in Barkingside I got into an argument with a very flash guy, and I said to one of my mates that I was going to do him. I told my mate to turn the lights off in the kitchen when this geezer went in there to get a drink. He did, and I caught the bloke with a sidekick in the knee when he walked through the door. When someone turned the lights back on, he was writhing in agony on the floor as his knee was broken.

Another time, I was in The Railway Tavern with my mates and met a gangly Irish youth at the bar. He told me he was a kung fu expert and then challenged me to a fight outside. We stood facing each other, he taking up a kung fu stance and me taking a Bushido stance. Then I suddenly flew at him with a kick to the chin and knocked him spark out.

That night, I was walking along Snakes Lane towards Woodford Station when I heard a car driving very fast behind me. I turned round just in time to see that it was heading straight for me. I picked up a scaffold pole that was lying in front of a house and hurled it at the windscreen, and then ran for my life. I later discovered that it was the Irish youth's older brother who was behind the wheel.

One of the hardest blokes in the area at the time was Jaffa, who was two years older than me. He was stockily built, with a hard-looking, lived-in face, and he always wore a long leather coat. He'd also been a skinhead, with the Wanstead crew. He was the life and soul of the party, always joking and talking at the rate of a hundred words a minute. Whenever we met, he'd greet me chirpily with, 'How you doing, bruv?' or 'What's up, bruv?'

His mum had died when he was five. At the age of eleven, he'd been sent to a Roman Catholic public school, where some of the priests and brothers had been very brutal to him. After becoming violent he was then sent to an approved school and then to Borstal. One time, he was banned from the High Street, Wanstead, after the Old Bill claimed he was demanding money with menaces from shopkeepers. When he needed to collect his laundry from a dry cleaner's in the High Street, he had to apply to court for permission. When he arrived at the station, the Old Bill were standing across the road waiting to escort him there, and his mates were watching, amused.

One Saturday afternoon, Jaffa, a couple of mates and I walked into The Red House pub to find it, unusually, full of pikeys (gypsies). We found a table in the corner and started playing cards. Jaffa was in one of his mad moods and he was looking for a fight.

'Listen,' I said to the other two guys when Jaffa went to the gents, 'it's going to go off soon, so you had better be ready.' I'd noticed the threatening looks we were getting from some of the pikeys. They both nodded.

The next minute I heard a commotion. Looking round, I saw Jaffa going hell for leather with three guys. I leapt out of my chair and went steaming in. Before I could whack anyone I was hit over the head with a bottle and I fell to the floor. I got back up straightaway, as more blokes joined in, and headed with Jaffa to the door. We didn't have a chance against so many of them.

Jaffa was the first geezer I'd seen use a knife. It happened when I went with him to the Plaza cinema in South Woodford one night. Some guy sitting in the seats behind began shouting at us.

'We'll have them outside,' said Jaffa, annoyed.

After the film finished, it all kicked off outside and Jaffa pulled a knife. When the guy tried to grab hold of the knife, Jaffa slashed his hands, cutting them to ribbons. The guy's girlfriend started screaming and banging her head against the lamppost. Jaffa and I then legged it and hid in a building site, worried that the Old Bill might come looking for us.

The first time I used a weapon was at a disco at Woodford Town Football Club one Saturday night. I'd gone there for a booze-up with John Hawkins. Halfway through the night he got into an argument with a bloke over something or other. The bloke was very lippy and was swearing at John. That's enough, I thought, getting angry. I drained the last drop of lager from the glass, leant over John's shoulder, and then smashed the glass over the bloke's head. The glass exploded and the guy collapsed across a table. I stood there holding the handle of the beer mug for a moment, wondering what to do. Then John and I pushed our way through the crowded dance floor to the doors and sprinted away.

When I got home, my adrenaline was still racing. I knew by glassing the guy I'd crossed a line, and by crossing that line I'd furthered my reputation on the streets.

Another night, I nearly got a pasting at a dance in a church hall in Woodford Bridge when I got into an argument with a guy and gave him a few slaps. He walked away and I thought no more about it. A few minutes later half a dozen Old Bill arrived from the nick opposite and one of them grabbed hold of me and gave me such a whack on the chin that he knocked me out. When I came round after a couple of minutes, an Old Bill put me up against a wall and said, 'We're going to take you to the cells and kill you.' I didn't know if he meant it, but I didn't want to stay around to find out, so when he released his grip I struggled free and legged it.

By now Laura and I were very much in love and we were talking about getting married and having children. But as her family were Jewish, she wasn't sure how they'd react. One day when I met her she told me that she had taken a home pregnancy test and that it was positive. I told her to double-check it with her GP. She did and he said, yes, she was pregnant. We were both over the moon.

We moved into the downstairs flat in a red-brick double-fronted Edwardian house in Seymour Gardens, between Redbridge and Ilford, and got married the following week, at Newbury Park Registry Office, on 14 February 1976, with Laura looking stunning in a green floral dress, and me looking very flash in a cream double-breasted suit with flared trousers. Soon after we were married I got a job as a plasterer's labourer.

In June, Laura was admitted to Wanstead Hospital to give birth. On the same day that she went in, I went with a mate to the White Hart. The deputy manager, who I knew quite well, allowed us to stay for a lock-in during the afternoon.

When the guv'nor, a bald, stocky geezer who wasn't worried about having a row, arrived back, I could tell that he was far from happy at finding us sitting at the bar.

'What's going on?' he asked the deputy as he went behind the counter.

'They're just having a late drink,' he answered.

'Not in my pub they're not,' said the guv'nor. He then turned to me and my mate and shouted, 'Out! Now!'

'Don't talk to me like that,' retorted my mate, eyeballing the guv'nor.

'I'll talk to you how I want,' he said, moving towards him. 'This is my pub. Now. Out!'

I wasn't having this, so I whacked the guv'nor in the mouth, knocking one of his teeth out. He staggered back, clutching his chin. We then drank up and walked out. As we reached the door, he shouted, 'You're barred.' We turned round and just laughed.

A couple of days later Laura gave birth to our first son, Adam. I was elated that I was a dad, and to celebrate his birth I went to have a few drinks with some mates at Woolston Hall. Afterwards, I caught a mini-cab to The White Hart, intending to teach the guv'nor a lesson. It was late at night and the street was deserted. I noticed a metal pole beside some roadworks, so I picked it up, hurled it through one of the pub's large windows, and walked off, laughing.

The next evening, a mate told me that the guv'nor was going to do the same to my house as someone had told him I'd done his window. I wasn't having this so, after visiting Laura and Adam in hospital, I caught the 235 bus to The White Hart and stormed into the public bar. Seeing me, some of the regulars looked up in surprise, as they knew I was barred.

'I hear you're going to do my house,' I said to the guv'nor across the bar.

He didn't reply and carried on wiping the glasses.

'Well, if you are, you're going to have to do me.' This was it. He was going to have a go at me now, I thought. 'If you want a row, let's have a row now.'

But instead he just muttered, 'Another time.'

'You'd better not do anything to my house,' I warned, and turned and walked back out of the pub.

He never did.

# 4

# In the Dock

Little did I know when I walked into the Room at the Top night club in Ilford that evening in the summer of 1977 that I was going to end up cutting a geezer and then find myself sitting in an interview room at Ilford nick a couple of days later, being grilled by two detectives.

'Now, Mr Mortlock, we want to know what happened outside the Room at the Top,' asked the first detective, sitting casually on the desk. He seemed young – not much older than me. It occurred to me briefly that our lives were heading in very different directions.

'Are you going to make a statement?' pressed the second one.

'No way,' I replied flatly.

'Well, you'd better see this then.' He threw a sheet of paper down on the desk.

It was a statement from Joe. I couldn't believe it – Joe had put me in the frame and said I'd cut the geezer. I'd always trusted Joe. I felt betrayed and angry, and knew Joe had done it to try and get off being charged with wounding.

'So, then, will you make a statement?' asked the younger one, getting off the desk.

'Okay. I was at the Room at the Top, having a night out, and a fight started when I came out. End of story.'

'That's it?'

'Yeah. That's it.' I shrugged.

'Listen. We know it's you,' he continued, pointing at my right hand. 'You're the only one who's cut. You cut yourself when you picked up the glass.'

'No. I've not done it. I'm left handed,' I lied.

I knew they weren't convinced. I was then charged with malicious wounding and two assaults, and given bail under my own security. I left the nick feeling worried about what might happen. The charges were serious, and I knew I might end up being sent down.

A few days later I was at a mate's house, drinking and playing cards, when Joe walked in. I could tell that he was surprised to see me.

'You're a grass,' I said angrily to him. I wanted to thump him, but because my right hand and arm were in plaster, I couldn't.

He shot me a nervous look. The next thing, one of my mates stood up and whacked him and Joe made a quick exit. Soon after, he was arrested for burglary and sent to prison on remand.

A few weeks later, Jaffa, John, Joe and I appeared at Redbridge Magistrates Court, where we pleaded not guilty to the charges. Ian had gone to ground since the fight and no one knew where he was. We were given bail and ordered to appear again a few weeks later.

By now, Laura was pregnant with our second baby. I knew that if I was sent down, life would be hard for her on her own. Despite this, my desire to fight remained as strong as ever. The night before I was due to appear again at Redbridge Magistrates Court for the committal hearing I went with Jaffa to a disco at Woodford Town Football Club. There was a guy there called Baz – small with long hair, he was a bolshy guy who didn't care about anything.

As the night went on, Baz started to become abusive and very loud. He then began to have verbal digs at Jaffa.

'Don't talk to him like that,' I said. The first time I'd used a weapon was there, at the football club, and I was thinking to myself that history was about to repeat itself.

'What's it to do with you?' he retorted.

That was it. I picked up a pint glass and brought it down on his head, but it didn't break. Baz swung at me and caught me on the chin with a punch, and I slammed my fist into his mouth. We ended up outside, having a real tear-up, and then Baz ran off up the road. As I stood there, wondering what to do, he reappeared, holding something in his hand. Another geezer was with him, and they advanced towards me. Baz had a cosh. He ran at me and smashed me across the face with it. I felt a searing pain run through me, and then drove my fist into the other geezer. Baz whacked me with the cosh again. Jaffa then came steaming in, but he was drunk and found it difficult to steady himself. At that point a third geezer joined in. Jaffa and I took a real hammering and we both ended up unconscious on the floor.

I woke up at about 3 a.m. in Whipps Cross Hospital, feeling sore and hardly able to move my jaw. Then I suddenly remembered that I was due in court later that morning, so I discharged myself and headed home.

At about 6.30 a.m. I was awoken by a banging on my door. Getting out of bed, I caught sight of myself in the mirror. I was shocked – I looked like the Elephant Man. I had two black eyes and my face was badly bruised and puffed up. I went downstairs and opened the door, wondering who it was.

It was a plain-clothes Old Bill. 'Can I come in?'

'Sure,' I said, and led him into the lounge.

'I know who's done this,' he said, sitting down. 'If you tell us who's done it, we'll nick him for grievous bodily harm with intent and he'll get four years.'

I shook my head. 'No. I'll sort it out myself.' I could hardly speak because of my jaw.

He leaned towards me. 'Now, if this carries on, one of your little firm is going to be lying on a slab with a ticket on his toe. And I don't want to do the paper work.'

Thinking that if the magistrate knew I'd been in a fight, it might go against me, I phoned Mr Brown, my solicitor, and told him we'd been in a car crash.

Because Jaffa was unable to turn up at court as he was still in hospital, the case was adjourned. Two weeks later, the four of us were committed for trial at Snaresbrook Crown Court. We were put on the warned list, which meant that we could be summoned to court at short notice. After the court hearing the Old Bill told us that we were also being charged with causing an affray. My heart sank when I heard this, as it increased the chances of us being sent down.

By this time I'd decided I was going to do Baz and the other guys, so the following week I went back to the football club with a mate. I told him to wait for me outside in the car and to keep the engine running. I wore a long leather coat with a carving knife concealed on the inside. I burst through the doors of the club, expecting to find Baz and the other guys at the bar.

'They're not here!' cried the manager, clearly worried by my presence.

'Well, where are they?'

'I don't know.'

In the end, through the grapevine, I arranged to meet Baz at The George in Wanstead to sort it out. I was expecting a real tear-up with him when Jaffa and I walked in there that night, but we were both ready for it. I spotted Baz sitting with a group of guys at a table by the fruit machine. We strode over to him. 'Right. Ready then?' I said, tensing myself.

'Sit down and have a drink,' he said, getting up and going to the bar.

I sat down, wondering what he was up to.

When he returned with the drinks, he said, 'Do you want to carry this on?'

'No. Do you?' I didn't see any point. We'd both given each other a good hiding.

'No.'

'Is it finished then?' I asked.

'Yeah. You know what, Al, you wouldn't go down.'

'How many times did it take then?' I asked.

'We had to whack you five or six times.'

I chuckled. 'Seriously?' We then spent the evening drinking together.

One Monday morning in September 1978, Jaffa, John and I arrived for the trial at Snaresbrook Crown Court. Joe arrived separately in a prison van, as he'd since been convicted of theft. We saw a few of the guys from the fight at the Room at the Top sitting on a bench with some Old Bill.

On the second day of the trial, the barrister representing Jaffa and me advised us to plead guilty. If we did, he said, we'd probably receive a three-year sentence, but if we didn't we'd be likely to get a stiffer sentence. He pointed out that affray carried a maximum of fourteen years, and malicious wounding the same.

'No way,' said Jaffa. 'We're going to fight it. It was self-defence.'

'Well, my advice is to plead guilty,' the barrister said.

'You're sacked,' retorted Jaffa.

'Yeah, we'll get another brief,' I said. I reckoned that the reason the barrister wanted us to plead guilty was because he was going to be in court for the Operation Countryman trial, the result of a major investigation into police corruption, which was due to begin that week, and he wanted our case out of the way.

'It's your decision,' said the barrister in an indifferent voice.

The judge adjourned the trial while my solicitor found us another barrister. At lunchtime we went to The Eagle pub across the road for a drink. We were in one bar and the jury in the other – I found this quite amusing.

The new barrister turned out to be a young, skinny guy with round glasses. With his black gown flowing, as he breezed into the cells below the court, he reminded me of Batman.

'I'll fight this case tooth and nail,' he announced confidently. 'I'm going to do my best to get you off. And if I can't, I'm going to get you the shortest sentence I can.'

After court that day, Jaffa came home with me and we sat up all night discussing what the outcome of the trial might be. We also took some time bombs – amphetamine-based tablets that make you feel very lively.

The new barrister put up a good defence, arguing that what we did after we came out of the Room at the Top was in self-defence. As I listened to him, I felt quietly confident that we would get off. When it came to my turn to go into the witness box to be cross-examined by the prosecution barrister, I felt nervous. I looked at the faces of the jury and thought to myself that they'd all be going home tonight, while my future hung in the balance.

I asked the judge if I could have a glass of water. He said I could, and the usher went out of the court to get one. When I took a sip, I caught sight of my dad, who was shaking his head at me and making a sign with his hands. What was the matter with him?

'Mr Mortlock, is it correct that you are left handed?' began the prosecution barrister.

'Yeah,' I replied.

'Do you do everything with your left hand?'

'Yeah.'

'Do you eat and drink with it?'

'Yeah, I do.'

'So you would hold a glass with your left hand?'

'That's correct.'

'So you would have no reason to hold anything in your right hand?'

'No.' What was he driving at?

'So why did you pick up that glass of water with your right hand?'

Thinking as fast as I could, I replied unconvincingly, 'Er, it was because it was given to me on my right-hand side.'

'Thank you, Mr Mortlock.' Pleased with himself, the prosecution barrister smiled smugly and sat down. 'No more questions, your honour.'

I knew I was in it now.

The judge sentenced Jaffa, John and Joe to twelve months in prison, adding that the two assault charges would be kept on file. When I heard this, my spirits rose as the first barrister had reckoned we'd all get at least three years. Given that I'd never been in a Borstal or detention centre, unlike Jaffa, John and Joe, I figured I might get off with a suspended sentence or probation.

Then the judge turned to me. He paused and fixed me with a steely gaze. 'I am sentencing you to eight months for the malicious wounding and eight months for the affray. The two sentences will run concurrently.' The two assault charges, relating to a couple of the geezers I'd whacked, were put on file.

I'd been given sixteen months inside, more than the others. I tried to let the words sink in. Prison. Sixteen months. I was twenty-two years of age. But compared to a possible three years or more, I knew really that it was a fair sentence. As I was taken down into the cells, I glanced across the court room at Laura and I saw tears running down her face.

When I reached the cell I said to a screw, 'How much have I got?'

'You've got eight months.'

'Eight months? I thought the judge said sixteen months.'

'No. Two eight-month sentences to run concurrently. That means together.'

'Well, that's a bit of a relief,' I said.

Jaffa, John and I were then handcuffed and led out of the back of the court to a green Ford Transit van for the journey to Wormwood Scrubs prison in west London. As the van drove along High Road, Leytonstone, I peered out of the barred window and saw The Green Man, The Crown and The Red Lion. Well, I'm not going to see these for a while, I thought to myself, becoming despondent.

'What's it like inside?' I asked Jaffa, who was reading a book called *The Profession of Violence*.

'You learn to get used to it, bruv.'

'Yeah?' I wasn't convinced. I wondered how I'd get used to being banged up in a cell and deprived of all the things I was used to. Yet despite the fact that I'd lose my freedom and wouldn't see Laura and Adam, a part of me began to see a spell in prison as adding to my reputation as a hard man.

# 5

# Banged Up

As we approached Wormwood Scrubs I thought how grim it looked in the gloomy September afternoon. How would I cope with life behind bars? I wondered. What's more, I was going to miss the birth of my second child. I tried not to think about that and reminded myself that I was only in for eight months, not three years. But sitting inside the prison van, eight months felt like eight years.

We were all booked in at the reception centre, where we had to undress, have our height and weight recorded, take a shower, and then put on prison clothes: blue jeans, a blue shirt and cheap shoes. There are four categories of prisoners: A, B, C and D. Category A is considered the most dangerous, and category D the least. I was classified as a category B prisoner. We were then taken to get some food. As I hadn't eaten since lunchtime, I was starving.

'This is all right, man. They do prawn balls here,' I said to Jaffa, when we reached the hot plate.

He laughed out loud. 'They're not prawn balls. They're roast potatoes.'

At about 9 p.m. we were taken to A wing. What struck me first was the smell. It was awful, a combination of food and disinfectant.

A screw unlocked a gate and ushered us through. Looking down the long wing, with cell doors on either side, I suddenly felt claustrophobic. The reality of prison really hit me. This was where I was going to live for the next eight months. I shuddered at the thought. We climbed up a metal staircase to the fourth floor landing, our footsteps making a loud clang, clang noise, and arrived at a cell.

'Right, you're in here tonight,' said the screw, opening the door.

The cell was tiny, about nine by six feet. It contained a bunk bed, table, chair and a pot. It was lit by a light built into the ceiling. High up at the far end was a small barred window.

I flinched when the screw slammed the cell door shut. 'Well, mate, I need some kip,' I said to Jaffa.

'And me,' he nodded, taking off his shoes and heaving himself on to the bottom bunk.

I climbed on to the top bunk and lay down. As I was used to two pillows, I rolled up the rough green blanket to make a second pillow. I thought of the events of the day and about Laura and Adam, but soon I drifted off to sleep, exhausted.

I was awoken in the morning by loud shouting, banging and clanking. It was deafening. I then noticed that the cell door was open and Jaffa's bed was empty. I went out on to the landing and stood there gobsmacked. What seemed like hundreds of men, all dressed in blue jeans and white shirts with thin blue stripes, and carrying bowls, buckets and trays, were running up and down the landing and the four metal staircases, as they made their way to the toilet, shower or hot plate. They reminded me of ants. I'd never seen anything like it.

I made my way down the stairs to the ground floor and joined the queue for the hot plate. But when I saw the food, my appetite disappeared. It looked disgusting. I returned to my cell with a tray containing a bowl of watery porridge and a mug of tea. Jaffa was sitting on the edge of his bed, smoking.

'Did you hear that noise this morning?' I said, sitting down on the chair and stirring the porridge.

'I know. That's one of the first things that hits you when you go inside. But you get used to it, Al.'

'Ugh! What, like the food?' I replied, spitting out the porridge. 'I can't eat this crap.'

'Well, mate, you'd better get used to it. It's all you're going to get. This ain't the Epping Forest Country Club.'

A short while later, a screw arrived and told us that we were being moved. Jaffa was given a cell on the third floor of A wing and I was given one on the second floor.

'Hi, mate.' A stocky-looking guy greeted me in a Liverpool accent when I entered the cell. 'I'm Chris.'

'I'm Alan,' I said, shaking his hand.

We chatted about this and that. He was a friendly guy who, I discovered, was finishing off a four-year sentence for cheque-book fraud and other scams.

Through the cell window I could see the visitors' gate, but watching people coming and going only heightened my sense of isolation.

A few days after this, I was moved to yet another cell. When I walked in, a burly bloke was lying on the top bed, smoking, and a pale-looking skinny guy with dirty straggly hair was sitting hunched up on the lower bed.

'How you doing?' said the burly bloke in an Irish accent.

'Okay, man,' I replied, wondering what was up with the skinny bloke. He looked a bit weird.

'Oh! The space rocket's here,' said the skinny bloke, getting up and going over to the window, which overlooked the kitchen. I could hear a lorry outside.

'Space rocket? What are you on about?' I said, exchanging glances with the Irish bloke.

The skinny bloke ignored me. The next minute he knelt down by the pot, had a pee, and then got back on his bed. Then he went to the window again and said excitedly, 'The space rocket's here.' This guy is very odd, I thought to myself. Then he had another pee and got back on his bed. He repeated these actions several more times. By now, he was driving me nuts.

'Listen, mate, don't do that again,' I shouted at him. 'Sit on the bed and don't move.'

He gave me a blank look, but did as I asked. Right, I thought, I'm not putting up with this guy, so I pressed the buzzer. A few minutes later a screw opened the cell door.

'What's the matter?' he asked.

'See him,' I said, pointing to the skinny guy, 'That's what the matter is. If he stays in this cell there's going to be grief.' I then explained what the skinny guy had done.

The screw reluctantly told the guy to get his gear together, and he then took him to another cell. In fact, he was moved to Jaffa and Joe's cell. A few hours later, when I was walking down the landing to get my lunch, I saw the skinny guy being taken out of his cell by the screws. There was blood everywhere.

'What's happened to him?' I asked Jaffa.

'Slashed himself,' he replied.

The prison day was long and monotonous. You'd get up at about 7 a.m. and then go and have a wash, use the toilet and slop out – in other words, empty the plastic bucket, which you'd peed in, down the sluice. Breakfast followed, either watery porridge or a fry-up caked in grease, and then you'd return to your cell. You were let out of your cell again at 1 p.m. to go down and collect your lunch and then you went back again. In the afternoon, weather permitting, you'd be allowed out in the yard, which had a high steel fence in front of the prison wall, for an hour. All you did was walk around with your mates, catching up on any gossip. After supper at 6 p.m. you were locked in your cell until the next morning.

I found it very hard to get used to being locked up for twenty-three hours a day, and nothing had really prepared me for the extreme boredom. I'd met a lot of blokes who had done bird and they'd told me how the days used to stretch out ahead monotonously, but I didn't really understand it. To occupy myself I read horror stories by Graham Masterson and James Herbert, wrote letters or drew pictures. Sometimes I'd do sit-ups and press-ups. One time, I even went to church, just to get out of the cell. I didn't go back, though, as it was so boring. The time in prison dragged incredibly slowly, and I realised why serving a prison sentence was described as 'doing time'. The occasions when you saw the door open or the spy hole open, you felt, somehow, a bit freer.

The way I coped with prison was to just think of it as a bit like working away from home. I used to lie on my bunk, thinking back to the trial, and wondering if I could have said something that would have got me off the charges.

One of the worst aspects of being cooped up in a tiny cell was if you had to use the pot in front of another inmate. There was an unwritten rule that you wouldn't have a crap in front of another prisoner because it would stink the cell out. Instead, you'd either press the bell and hope a screw would let you use the toilets on the landing or simply hold it in. One time, Chris told me he had to go immediately, in the cell, so I buried my head in the mattress.

I was given a job on the hot plate, serving the food. Because of this I was moved to a cell on the ground floor of C wing. My new cell mate was called Del, who was from Stratford, just down the road from me, and who was also in for violence. He was about the same age as me and had long Jason King-type ginger hair, a droopy moustache, and he wore gold-rimmed glasses.

Working on the hot plate meant that I could help myself to things such as leftover food, sugar and milk. It was one of the perks of the job. The screws knew this went on, but they turned a blind eye. One day, a well-known East End face asked me if I could get him some rice pudding from the hot plate. No problem, I replied, and told him to meet me on the landing after exercise.

When he turned up, I gave him the plastic container full of rice pudding. He looked at it suspiciously.

'What's the matter?' I asked.

'You haven't spat in it, have you?'

'No. Why?' I was shocked that he thought I might do this, but I knew what he was talking about. I'd heard stories about some of the guys in the kitchen spitting or peeing into vats of soup and other food.

'That's okay then. Cheers,' he said and went back to his cell.

In prison you learn to be very resourceful in order to get round the rules and regulations. For example, some inmates lit cigarettes using a tin, a flint and some wadding material. They'd flick the flint and the spark would ignite the wadding. To heat up cold water you attached a razor blade to a piece of electric flex, which connected to the light socket, and then you dangled the blade in the water. And if I wanted to make toast, I'd fill a dustpan with tissues, light it, and then hold a piece of bread above the flames.

I'd read in the *Ilford Recorder*, which Laura used to send me each week, that the guy I'd cut outside the Room at the Top had been nicked for something else. If he was found guilty, I knew that there was a good chance he might be sent to the Scrubs. I told this to Jaffa during exercise and we started making plans to do him if he arrived. We scanned all the new prisoners each week, but he never came.

Soon after, I was informed that, along with Del, I was going to be moved to Camp Hill on the Isle of Wight to finish my sentence. Although I'd be farther away from Laura, I was pleased about the move because the regime down there was meant to be a lot more lax than at the Scrubs and they were supposed to have a good gym. On the other hand, I'd also heard that they'd had some serious race riots there, so I was a bit apprehensive.

One morning, Del and I were taken by a screw to the wing office, where we were told that the next day we were in fact going to be moved to Wandsworth instead of Camp Hill. Wandsworth had a reputation as a very strict, violent prison, where the prison officers beat you up. But, I just thought to myself, well, if I have to go there, I have to go, and that's it.

Del, however, was petrified at the prospect of being sent to Wandsworth, so he asked me to cut his hair short so that he'd look tougher. I'd made a bit of a name for myself as a barber in prison, and I was allowed to use a pair of scissors and a comb that were locked in a metal box in the wing office. Each time, though, I had to sign for them, in case they went missing.

The following morning, Del and I took our belongings to the reception area, where we changed into our suits, and waited for the van to take us to Wandsworth. We sat there for three hours, wondering what the delay was. Then a screw told us that we weren't going to Wandsworth because the screws there had gone on strike and they wouldn't accept any new prisoners. Instead, he said, we'd probably be sent to Camp Hill in a few days. When I heard this, I felt relieved.

A week later, along with half a dozen other prisoners, I was handcuffed and put in a small coach for the journey to Camp Hill. I was handcuffed to Micky Mannion, a short, stocky guy with short cropped blond hair and a moustache. He was an armed robber from south London.

On the ferry from Portsmouth one of the blokes, observing his handcuffs, asked a screw, 'What if the ferry sinks?'

'You swim in pairs,' replied the screw dryly.

I laughed when I heard this, but the bloke had a point. What would happen if the ship sank? Thankfully, the journey to the Isle of Wight was only about half an hour.

Camp Hill was at the top of a steep hill in Newport. Below it were two other prisons, Parkhurst and Albany. Camp Hill is mainly for prisoners reaching the end of their sentences, while Parkhurst and Albany are, generally, for long-term prisoners. Whereas Wormwood Scrubs was a traditional Victorian prison, Camp Hill was laid out very differently. It consisted of a number of separate blocks, each containing about fifty cells on two landings.

Micky and I were put in a cell in the block in an old part of the prison for the first week. This meant that you were only allowed out of your cell to get your food. I think they did this with new arrivals so as to make an impression on you. But having already been locked up for twenty-three hours a day in the Scrubs, being in the block made no impression on me.

I could see that Micky was getting very agitated because he hadn't seen his wife for a few weeks or received any letters.

'You want to spar?' he asked out of the blue one morning.

'What?' I replied, knowing that his mind was all over the place and that he was a dangerous guy. *And* he was about four stone heavier than me.

'Do you want to spar? We can wrap towels around our hands.'

'Okay then.' Here we go, I thought, he wants a tear-up. We wrapped our hands in towels and faced each other.

'No hitting in the face,' said Micky.

'You ready,' I replied, squaring up. The first thing Micky did was to punch me in the face. I then landed him one on his chin, and we both really went at it. From then on, we started to spar regularly, partly to relieve the monotony of prison life and partly to keep in shape.

After a week, I was taken to a cell in St Thomas's wing, a modern, square building. There were three blokes in the cell, and I didn't like the look of two of them. I could tell that these two were bully boys. After I'd unpacked, I climbed on to the top bunk and sat there rolling a cigarette. I had decided that there was no way I was going to let them intimidate me.

'Anyone want a fag?' I asked, looking around.

'Yeah, cheers, mate,' said one of the bully boys, coming over to me. I could see he was surprised by my offer.

'Where do you come from?' he asked, taking a paper and the tobacco pouch.

'East London.'

'So, who do you know there?'

'Quite a few people,' I replied, carrying on rolling my cigarette.

'Such as?'

I've never been one for dropping names, but I felt in this situation it wouldn't go amiss. So I mentioned the name of one very heavy villain I knew and they both went quiet. After that, they were fine with me and, in fact, we became quite good mates. To pass the time, we used to do some weight lifting together in the cell, using containers of water tied on to broom handles.

Camp Hill turned out to be a more relaxed regime than the Scrubs. The food was better and you weren't banged up in your cell for twenty-three hours a day – we were let out more often and allowed to walk around the wing and also to wander in and out of other prisoners' cells.

I was put in an outside working party. My job was to cut the grass and weed the pavements of the houses of the screws who worked in Albany, but I didn't really like it because it made me feel like a servant. The only good thing was that one of the screws from the Albany would give you tobacco for a roll-up.

I became friends with Keith, a well-built Greek guy who was covered in tattoos, and we started to train in the gym together. He wore a red arm band, which signified that he was a trusted prisoner. He knew I wasn't happy with the gardening party, so he used to ask for me to help him out in the gym. Up until then, I'd never done any weight lifting, and when I first went to pick up a set of weights I was amazed at how heavy they were. I couldn't even lift them an inch off the ground.

A month or so later I was moved to another cell on the landing above, and found myself sharing with a guy called Little Nicky, who used to draw pictures of prisoners' wives and families, Winny, a fat, red-faced guy who reminded me of a penguin, and Jock, a quiet Scotsman who only had a month to go before his release.

All the while, I knew that Laura was finding life hard at home, even though she never complained in her letters. Our second baby was due in a few weeks and money was tight. She'd sold some stamp albums that her grandfather had given her to get a bit of money for Christmas. I was gutted that she only got a hundred quid for them, as one of the albums had a Penny Black and a Penny Red in it.

One day, I heard that a firm who thought they ran the wing were going to cut Paul, a guy on my working party who was in for robbery. They didn't like him because he was black. Although the racial tensions I'd heard about had been largely sorted out, most of the black guys tended to stick together. The plan was to do Paul at the weekly film on Friday in the old gymnasium. I knew that in prisons people were often cut during film showings because it was dark; a favourite weapon was a razor blade welded to a toothbrush.

So I warned Paul to watch his back, and he thanked me and said he'd be prepared. When Friday evening came, Paul turned up at the old gymnasium with a dozen black guys, and the other blokes bottled out.

The same firm used to supply tobacco. For example, if you borrowed a quarter of an ounce, you had to pay back half an ounce. One day, I asked Little Nicky to ask the firm to lend me a quarter of an ounce, as I'd run out of tobacco. But I had no intention of paying it back.

The following week Little Nicky came up to me one day in the TV room and said that this firm wanted their tobacco repaid. 'Tell them they're knocked,' I replied, tapping my chest. This meant that I wasn't going to repay them.

A short while later he returned. 'They're going to do you,' he said.

'I'm not worried about them,' I said nonchalantly. I was confident that my mates and I could handle them. 'If they want some, tell them they can have some.'

The next day I was practising on the darts-board on my own in the recreation room when half a dozen guys walked in.

'Mortlock,' one of them called out.

'Yeah,' I casually answered as I carried on throwing the darts.

'We've a little bit of business to sort out.'

'Is that right?' I said, turning round. The six of them were standing in a line in front of the door. I might have been outnumbered, but I had a weapon. I pulled the darts out of the board and held them in one hand with the tips pointing towards them. 'Okay, then. Come on.'

But not one of them made a move, and they turned around and walked back out. As they left, one of them called, 'When you come up on the landing we're going to do you.'

'Yeah, all right,' I snarled.

'You'll see,' he sneered.

I then went into the TV room, where Paul and some of his black mates were sitting. I wanted to make sure I had some back-up if this firm had a go at me before Keith and the others returned.

'That firm who wanted you now want to do me. Watch my back, will you? Keith and the others aren't back yet,' I whispered as I sat down next to Paul.

'No problem, man,' he said, standing up and signalling to his mates to do the same.

'No. It's okay for the moment,' I said.

I left the TV room and hung around in the corridor near the tea urn waiting for Keith, Little Nicky and Winny to return. After a while they all came back, and I told them what had happened and that we needed to sort out this firm. They were all up for it.

While Keith went up to his cell and got a couple of batteries and put them inside two socks, I went to Johnny's cell. Johnny was an armed robber with a big reputation. When I explained what we were planning to do, he said he was up for it, and put on his boots. The five of us then went up on to the next landing in search of the firm. Seeing what we were doing, one of the screws went to press the alarm for back-up.

'There's no need for that,' I called. I knew him quite well. He always reminded me of Postman Pat because he always wore his cap with the peak pushed up.

'You sure?'

I nodded. 'We've got it sorted.'

We saw one of the firm standing outside a cell; he looked nervous as we approached. Johnny grabbed hold of him by the shoulders and shoved him into the cell. Keith then stormed into the cell and we followed him. 'Okay. You want it?'

The blokes just stood there, shaking their heads. 'No,' said the biggest one.

Satisfied that we'd made our point, we then walked out and went back to our landing.

I became popular as a tattooist while at Camp Hill. I was quite good at it and had tattooed a lot of my mates in east London. I'd ask some prisoners doing art classes to nick me a bottle of Indian ink and then get a needle and cotton from one of the screws on the pretext of wanting to sew my trousers. I'd then draw a picture with a ballpoint pen, tie the cotton around the end of the needle, dip it into the Indian ink, and jab the skin. I could only do it when the screws weren't around as the prison authorities didn't allow tattooing, and it took ages, but then again we all had a lot of time on our hands. I never got caught. I'd get paid with biscuits or chocolate.

At 6 a.m. one cold December morning I heard the cell door opening. Rubbing the sleep from my eyes, I looked up to see a screw standing there.

'Mortlock,' he barked.

'What?'

He smiled. 'Your wife's had a little boy.'

'Yeah?' I replied, trying to take in the news.

'And they're both as good as gold.'

'Cheers, mate.'

I felt a wave of joy surge through me; I was a dad again. But the joy subsided when I reminded myself that I still had another three months to serve.

Just after Christmas, I was lying on my bunk on a Sunday morning when a screw walked into the cell.

'Mortlock.'

'Yeah,' I replied.

'Get yourself dressed.'

'Why?'

'You've got a visitor.'

'Who?'

'Your missus.'

'Don't be silly.' Laura always wrote to tell me when she was coming to see me.

'Come on. Get yourself together.'

I leapt off the bunk, put on a clean shirt and trousers, and excitedly followed the screw to the visiting room. I was stunned when I saw Laura sitting there with a navy blue carry-cot on her knee.

She was beaming. 'Do you want to hold him, Al?'

'Of course I do,' I laughed, giving her a kiss and taking him in my arms and cradling him. He felt so soft.

'How did you get here, luv? They say this is the worst winter for years.'

'It was a nightmare. I had to catch a cab to the tube station, then the tube to Waterloo, then a train to Portsmouth, the ferry, and then a bus to the bottom of the hill near the prison. But I wanted you to see Jamie.'

'Well, love, thanks for making the effort,' I said, holding her hand. 'He's lovely. Just like his dad.' Laura laughed, and then handed me the bottle to feed him.

Immediately after the visit, I felt elated, but when I got back to my cell I felt gutted. Not for the first time I began to think back to the tear-up that night in llford, and I wished I'd gone home and not got involved. I'd missed the birth of my second son, as well as Christmas, and I'd miss my wedding anniversary and birthday. I resolved to make sure I never ended up in prison again. I had to remember that I'd a wife and children to take care of.

As the day of my release approached, I felt worried that I might be arrested at the gates. I'd heard that it was not uncommon for the Old Bill to arrest some prisoners with fresh charges as soon as they walked out, and I remembered that the judge had said that the two assault charges would stay on file. When I spoke to a screw about it, he told me I'd nothing to worry about. I hoped he was telling the truth and not just saying it to make me feel better.

I was so excited the night before my release that I couldn't sleep. I just couldn't wait to be back with Laura, Adam and Jamie, see my mates again, have decent food, and be able to go for a drink again.

I was released from Camp Hill on 19 February 1979, and as I came out of the gates Laura was waiting for me. She'd come down the day before and spent the night in a hotel. We hugged each other.

'I'll tell you what, Laura.'

'What, Al?'

'I'm never coming to the Isle of Wight for a holiday, that's for sure.'

She burst out laughing and linked her arm through mine. 'Come on. Let's catch the ferry and get back home.'

# 6

# Drug Wars

Back home in east London and free again, my first problem was getting some money. My financial situation was so bad that the phone had now been cut off. But, given the amount of building work going on in and around London in 1979, I felt confident that something would turn up.

One day, I saw an advert in the *Evening Standard* for an under-pinner, someone who digs tunnels under a house when the founda-tions have crumbled. So I went to my 'office' – the phone box at the end of the street – and phoned up the company. When they asked me if I was experienced I said that I was, but in reality I'd only ever done one underpinning job. I felt, though, that what I didn't know I'd soon pick up.

The following week, I started the job and found myself working with two pikeys, who had given up the travelling life and were now living in houses in Rochford in Essex. We all got on really well together, and although the work was hard, I was earning good money – about 250 quid a week.

The Valentine became my local. Situated opposite the Odeon at Gants Hill, it was a big traditional pub with a mock Tudor front. One of the bars had pool tables in it and replica guns on the wall. All the Irish builders used to drink in the public bar, and in the saloon bar you'd get everyone – from Hell's Angels and greasers, to villains and accountants. It was a crazy place. Talking to various blokes there, I discovered that since I'd been in prison there'd been a lot of violent incidents involving different firms in the Ilford area, and no one seemed to know what was behind it.

With some money in my pocket again, I felt I was putting my life back together, but I couldn't escape my past. One evening I was having a drink in The White Hart in Woodford Bridge with a mate when a guy called Charlie started giving me a lot of lip because I'd been in prison. He was saying things like, 'Oh, I bet you think you're hard now because you've been inside.' I started to get annoyed with him, and when he went to the gents I followed him. I waited until he reached the corridor between the public and saloon bars and then got stuck into him, releasing a flurry of kicks at his chest and head. I was unstoppable. Eventually, some of the regulars pulled me off.

Afterwards, I went to my mate's house. We hadn't been there long when a guy called Micky phoned and asked to speak to me. He was a boxer and had a big reputation in the area, and I knew that he was a mate of the bloke I'd had a row with.

'Hello, Mortlock. How are your legs?' he asked in a menacing voice. This was a term that was sometimes used to tell someone that you were going to shoot them in the legs.

'My legs are all right, but if you keep on, yours won't be,' I said, slamming the phone down. An hour later, I heard a car pull up outside. The next thing, the garden was engulfed in flames – someone had lobbed a firebomb over the fence. This is getting nasty, I thought. Word soon went round that Micky was going to try to do me.

Not long after, I was in The Valentine with Jaffa, who, like me, was finding it hard to escape his past. A few days after being released from prison he'd thrown a crash helmet through his step-mother's front window and then barricaded himself in her garage. She called the Old Bill and Jaffa ended up attacking them with an axe, screwdriver and other weapons. They sent in the Old Bill dogs, who leapt up at Jaffa and bit him. He bit one of them back. He was eventually arrested, charged, convicted of various offences, and sent to Brixton prison.

He appealed and, after a few weeks in Brixton, he was given two suspended sentences. Jaffa was now working the doors at clubs and pubs in south London with Cass Pennant, a big, tough, black guy who had been one of the leaders of West Ham United's notorious Inter City Firm.

One evening, Jaffa and I walked into The Valentine, both wearing our long leather coats. Micky and another guy were sitting at a table in the corner.

'Right, I'm going to sort this,' I said to Jaffa.

'What you going to do?'

'I'm going to front him out.'

I stood up and walked over to Micky at the bar. Jaffa followed me.

'Do you want to sort this out?' I said.

'Yeah,' he replied.

'Okay.'

'Why are you getting involved in Charlie's battles? I had a straightener with him and gave him a good hiding. Can't he look after himself?'

He paused. 'Maybe you're right. Want a drink?'

I was taken aback. 'Okay.'

'Well, I ain't going to need this then, am I?' he said, giving it the big 'un and pulling out a bricklayer's trowel from his coat pocket.

Then Jaffa said, 'And I ain't going to need this either,' as he pulled out a large bayonet from the inside of his coat.

I worked on demolition sites, tearing roofs off, driving the dumper, working the jackhammer machine, and breaking concrete with a sledgehammer. I even helped to knock down the Wilkinson Sword factory in Acton and whole streets of houses all over London.

There was a crane with a large ball attached to it by long chains. I used to stand on the ball and hold on to the chain, and the crane driver, Bernie, would lift it and take me to the top of a building. One day, a couple of us were working on the top of the Co-op in Stratford. We were perched on a ledge and cutting away a steel girder with an acetylene torch. Suddenly the building began to vibrate, and I looked down to see Bernie smashing the ball into it.

'Bernie! Stop! Stop!' I screamed down to him. He's still hung over from the night before, I thought to myself, but he remained expressionless and carried on swinging the ball into the building. Any minute now, I thought, we were going to fall thirty feet off the ledge. Then I saw the owner of the company running frantically across the site towards the crane. He hauled himself up into the cab and switched off the crane.

I was becoming unhappy working for other people and I wanted to be my own boss. When I walked from my flat in Seymour Gardens to The Valentine I used to pass a house that always had a couple of cars for sale in the drive. A large orange sign that said 'Cars for Sale' hung above the front door. I was pointing the brickwork on the roof of the Tizer factory in Tottenham one afternoon when I thought to myself, *I* could do up cars like this bloke.

When I was on my way to a job in Ascot, Surrey, one morning, I noticed a garage in a village I passed through had a Ford Escort for sale for ninety-five quid. I told the bloke I was with to stop the truck while I had a look at the car. After a bit of haggling, I managed to persuade the garage owner to let me have it for sixty-five quid. Because I didn't have a driving licence, a bloke I knew drove the car up to Ilford for me. I then filled the holes up with filler, resprayed it, placed an advert in the *Ilford Recorder*, and sold it for one hundred and seventy quid. I also began doing up Volkswagen Beetles, which I bought from Flash Harry who had a stack of them in a yard in Hainault in Essex. This is an easy way of earning money, I thought, and before long I was selling a few cars a month.

I was looking through the local paper one day and my eye was caught by an advert offering classes in Modka, meaning modern karate. This was full contact karate. It left out a lot of the traditional Japanese moves and replaced them with a more kick-boxing approach. I really fancied this and the following week I went down to join the classes, which were held in a church hall in Colworth Road, Leytonstone. The instructor was Carl Nelson. I learnt that he was originally from Tiger Bay in Cardiff and that he hadn't got into martial arts until he was in his forties. He'd learnt his karate from Ticky Donovan, a leading instructor from Dagenham, who had coached the English karate team. I found Modka quicker and tougher than traditional karate, but I took to it very easily.

Around this time, I met a bloke called Barry the Hat, who was a bit like the Arthur Daley character in the TV series *Minder*. He drove an old Ford Corsair and often wore a white safari suit and white hat as he'd just returned from South Africa, where he'd been working. Like me, he was a ducker and diver and was always coming up with scams. He told me he'd been asked to build an extension to a snooker club in Gants Hill and he offered me labouring work. He was paying well, so I took it. We became good mates and started going boozing together. In fact, some people started calling us Arthur and Terry, the names of the two leading characters in *Minder*.

One afternoon a guy knocked on the door of my flat and asked me if I had a plaster, as he'd cut his finger. He told me his name was Steve White and that he had just moved into the flat upstairs. Tall with short hair, he seemed a very confident guy. He was quite flash and often wore silk shirts open at the top to reveal a gold medallion. He drove an enormous burgundy Chevrolet Monte Carlo.

I got to know him over the next few weeks and discovered that he was dealing in, and smuggling, drugs. I'd suspected this because of the number of people I saw coming and going from his flat at all hours. He or his couriers used to go to Africa for what appeared to be a holiday and return with kilos of cannabis hidden in luggage. One time when he was in Ghana, soldiers turned up at his hotel in the middle of the night and arrested him. At one point, he was blindfolded, put in a car, and driven to a building somewhere. He discovered the next day from another prisoner that some of the soldiers had wanted to shoot him, but others had argued with them not to. He spent five weeks in prison before the British Embassy negotiated his release. Not long after he moved in, Customs and Excise raided his flat and he was sent to Brixton prison on remand.

I used to buy and sell drugs in the Valentine, along with a few other pubs in the area, such as The Red Lion in Romford Road and The Angel in High Road, Ilford. Tony, the landlord of The Valentine, knew about the drug dealing and he wasn't too happy about it, but he never tried to put an end to it. The Old Bill knew what was going on and raided the pub several times.

We didn't do the deals in a blatant fashion, however. The drugs would usually be sold in a quiet corner of the pub or outside in the car park. When people were going off clubbing they would often stop off at The Valentine for some gear. Back then, cocaine cost sixty quid a gram, while speed only cost a tenner. I'd buy, say, an ounce of speed for a hundred quid and then cut it into packages and sell them to people in the pub for a tenner each. I'd make about four hundred quid. I used to buy the gear off a mate who lived in a flat on a council estate in Dalston.

Although I regularly took speed, I'd never taken heroin, nor had I ever wanted to. Because they relied on regular fixes and would do anything to get that, I saw heroin users as weak people. One Sunday afternoon, I was having a few drinks in a mate's house when he put two mirrors on the table and then tipped some white powder on to both of them. I sniffed some powder from one of the mirrors, thinking it was coke, but it turned out to be Chinese white heroin. I thought I was going to die and ended up unconscious. I was sick all night and still felt dreadful the next day. I never took it again.

One evening I went to The Valentine. Standing at the bar was a bloke called Georgie Dice, who I thought might have a bit of gear. A big guy with short, dark hair, he was dressed in a leather jacket and jeans.

Fancying a bit of speed, I said to him, 'Got any billy, mate?'

'Here. Take this,' he said, handing me a small bag from his pocket.

'You sure?'

'Yeah. Take it.'

After that, Georgie and I became good mates and we started drinking regularly together. He was a good snooker player and also loved poker. He was nicknamed Georgie Dice because he used to play dice a lot.

Danny and Keith used to sell drugs for me in the Valentine. Danny was a smart guy who was more into the business side of things than having a tear-up. Keith was black and looked a bit like Sammy Davis Junior. He was five feet tall and had a wonky eye, a slight limp, and a humped back. He was one of the most dangerous characters I'd ever met. He'd not long been out of prison after stabbing a bloke with a kitchen knife.

I remember being in a pub with him once when he put some money down on the side of the pool table. This was so that he could have the next game. The blokes who were playing started taking the mickey out of him because he looked a bit odd. I watched the situation from the bar, thinking to myself, these guys don't know what they're getting into. And sure enough, Keith suddenly erupted. He grabbed a pool cue and, wielding it like a cricket bat, smashed one of the geezers in the face with the thick end. The bloke's teeth flew through the air, then Keith grabbed one of the other guys, yanked him through the doors, and beat him senseless outside. When he came back into the pub, he had a bandage around his head.

''Ere, mate, you look like a bleedin' Sikh,' I laughed. Keith smiled, gave me a playful punch in the chest, and told me to get him another drink. He respected me and we liked each other.

One hot Friday night in July, Laura and I went for a night out. By this time, our third son, Sean, had been born. After a couple of drinks at The Valentine, we went to The Red Lion in Romford Road, where I'd arranged to pick up some money from Keith and Danny. After ordering our drinks at the bar we went outside and found an empty table in the beer garden. We'd only been there a few minutes when a lean-looking bloke with a rugged face, in a suit, came up to me.

'You doing the gear in here, mate?'

'What's it got to do with you?' I replied, tensing a little but remaining calm.

'I said you're selling the gear, mate, ain't you?' he repeated.

'So what,' I said, studying him closely. What was all this about? The next thing, Keith appeared from nowhere. 'Who do you think you're talking to?' he challenged the geezer. 'Don't talk to him like that.'

The other geezer just laughed and told him to eff off. I knew what was coming. Then, as quick as lightning, Keith picked up Laura's gin and tonic glass and slashed the geezer's neck. Blood spurted everywhere and the geezer staggered back, clutching his neck in agony. Screams from women filled the air and people leapt up from the tables, scattering in different directions. Looking at the geezer writhing in agony, all I could think of was the bloody image of a man on the cover of a video called *The Howling*.

I knew we had to get away quickly, as there was a nick just across the road. Laura, Keith, Danny and I swiftly left and jumped on the first bus that came along. We ended up in The Ruskin Arms in High Street North, East Ham. The Ruskin was a well-known pub in the area, as it had a boxing gym upstairs and it was also a major venue for rock bands. Iron Maiden had begun their career here.

I took Keith into the gents to examine his hands. They were cut to ribbons, and his white tracksuit was covered in blood.

'Get your socks off,' I ordered.

'My socks?'

'Yeah, I'm going to bandage your hands with them.' I carefully wrapped the socks around his hands, and then we went back into the bar and spent the rest of the evening drinking. We weren't worried about what had happened at The Red Lion. It was just another ruck. I was more concerned with finding out who the geezer was and what he was up to. I felt that Keith might have badly injured him or even killed him. I told Keith there was no way he could go to hospital because he would be nicked, and that I'd try and sew up his hands when we got home.

When we got to the flat, Keith took his bloodstained clothing off and Laura put it in the washing machine. We all stayed up that night taking more speed and trying to put the incident at the Red Lion out of our minds. When Keith left at dawn I told him that we'd have to listen to what the word was on the street about the geezer he'd slashed.

Later that afternoon, Danny turned up at the flat. 'The Old Bill have nicked Keith,' he said. 'Someone at The Red Lion told the Old Bill that a small black guy did it,' he went on.

With Keith's distinctive appearance and reputation for violence, the Old Bill would have known straightaway that he was the bloke. 'Has my name been mentioned?' I asked.

'No, but they know you were there.'

A couple of days later, I was at my mate Mick's house in Hainault when Barry the Hat turned up at the door at about 3 a.m., jumping up and down and looking very worried.

'You've got trouble, big trouble, Al,' he said, as he bustled into the living room.

'What do you mean?'

'I've been looking everywhere for you. Then I thought, I'll try Mick's as a last resort.'

'Why? What's up?' I asked impatiently.

'That geezer who Keith cut, do you know who he was?'

'Ain't got a clue, Barry. Never seen him before,' I replied.

'Well, he's with a Romford firm, and they're very naughty. They're into protection and I've heard they've no qualms about topping anyone who gets in the way.'

I was taken aback. For some reason, it hadn't occurred to me that the geezer might be connected in any big way. I thought he was probably some two-bit dealer chancing his arm. But this information didn't worry me. I figured that clashing with them would give me a bigger reputation.

'Yeah,' continued Barry, 'they turned up in an orange Volvo at The Red Lion last night and they were asking everyone where you were. Someone saw a geezer sitting in the back of the car with a harpoon gun.'

The following lunchtime I was having a drink in the Valentine when a small geezer I hadn't seen before came over to me at the bar. He told me he hadn't long been out of prison and that he was the brother of a well-known armed robber I'd been in Camp Hill with. I wasn't too sure about him, but I bought him a drink anyway.

'Did you hear about the geezer who got cut at The Red Lion?' he asked.

'Yeah? Who got cut then?' I said, feeling that this bloke knew something about the Red Lion incident. Who was he? Old Bill? A grass? Or was he connected to this Romford firm?

'A bloke who's related to a very naughty firm?'

'Is that right.'

'Yeah. I hear you've got a little bit of trouble.'

'What do you mean, a little bit of trouble? No. I ain't got no trouble.'

'That's what I heard.'

'What you got to do with this firm then?'

'I know them.'

'Yeah.'

'They're the type of geezers who will come through your doors in the middle of the night and do your wife and kids.'

'That right?'

'Take it from me. You want to watch your back,' he answered.

I saw the bloke several times in The Valentine that week. One afternoon, he came over to me and said, 'They want to have a meet with you.'

'Who?'

'The firm from Romford.'

'What do they want a meet for?'

'They want to get it sorted.'

'Where do they want to meet?'

'I'll find out and let you know this evening.'

I saw him again that evening and he told me the firm wanted a meet in Romford.

'I ain't meeting on their manor,' I said. 'Tell them to meet me in McDonald's in Ilford at 2 p.m. on Saturday.' I knew McDonald's would be packed and that this firm would be less likely to pull out any tools there. I'd have my boys plotted up both inside and outside the restaurant.

I went home and told Laura about what had happened. She'd seen me in a few sticky situations and just accepted that it went with the territory. But this was different. No one had ever threatened her and the kids before.

'Alan, what are we going to do? What about the children?'

'Don't worry about it. I'll make sure they don't get in here. Trust me.' I said, giving her a hug. 'It'll be okay.'

We'd moved from the ground floor flat to the upstairs flat. This meant that if these blokes turned up they couldn't get through the windows. I decided to booby trap the main door by leaning six foot weight lifting bars up against it. This was so that the noise would alert me if someone tried to break in.

I had a big hammer and some knives in the flat, but I realised they might not be enough if this firm turned up. I knew what I needed: a gun. I'd been around geezers with guns before, although I'd never used one.

I phoned Barry the Hat. 'Barry, I need a piece.'

'No problem, Al. I'll get it sorted.'

However, before I received the gun, events took a dramatic turn. Worried about the safety of Laura and the kids, I asked my dad if I could borrow his caravan in Maldon, Essex, for a few days. A mate lent me his Ford Escort Mexico. Early on the morning we were due to leave, Laura went around to the laundrette.

'Alan, there's police everywhere down the road!' she said when she returned. 'Something must have happened.'

'Yeah?' I replied, unconcerned, and carried on packing the kids' clothes.

Before we left for Maldon I had to collect some money from a geezer who I'd sold bent MOTs to, so I got in the car and drove off down the street. Suddenly, an Old Bill motor pulled out in front of me and blocked my way forward. I tried to drive around it, but the next thing I knew was that I was surrounded by Old Bill pointing guns at me.

'Get out of the car! And don't move,' one of them shouted.

I slowly got out and put my hands in the air, wondering what the hell was going on. Above, I could hear the drone of a helicopter. I was then slung over the bonnet of the car. Out of the corner of my eye I saw the nozzle of a gun against my head. It was a .38 Smith and Wesson – I remember noticing what a lovely grain of wood there was on the handle. Then I saw that the hand holding it was shaking. I just hope he doesn't sneeze, I thought.

I was then handcuffed and frog-marched down the road back to the flat. By now, all the neighbours had come to their doors and windows. I remember the look of amazement on Laura's face when she opened the door to find me handcuffed and surrounded by armed police. The Old Bill turned the house over, but Laura refused to let them into the children's rooms because they were carrying guns.

'I'm arresting you on suspicion of possessing firearms,' said the inspector eventually.

I was thankful that Barry had not yet got me the gun. I kept calm and told Laura to ring my solicitor. As I was being bundled into the back of the Old Bill motor, I saw a lorry with some of my builder mates coming down the road. It then braked sharply, did a U-turn and sped off, pursued by an Old Bill motor. It was quite funny really, like something out of *The Keystone Cops*. The Old Bill obviously thought my mates were in the frame.

At Ilford nick I was thrown in a cell. When my solicitor arrived, he told me that the Old Bill thought that there was a gun, but didn't know where it was. He added that they wanted to do some quick-fire questions and answers with me. Fine, I said, having decided I was going to say nothing to them anyway. I knew I had nothing to worry about as they couldn't have had any evidence against me, so I decided to just relax.

I was taken into an interview room, where a surly chief inspector was sitting at the table and two detectives were leaning up against the wall with their arms folded.

'I'm Chief Inspector Smith from the Serious Crime Squad,' he said. 'The first question I want to ask you, Alan, is this: are you in fear of your life?'

'No,' I replied casually.

'Well, we believe that you are.'

'And I'm telling you I'm not,' I said firmly.

'Where's the shotgun and the six rounds of ammunition?' he asked.

'I don't know what you're talking about. I don't own a gun. I don't even own an air rifle.'

The questions continued, but I refused to give anything away. In the end, the chief superintendent was really needled.

'All I'm telling you is that we know what's going on in Ilford,' he said. 'Now, listen to me.' He paused, leant across the table, and stared hard at me. 'If there's any gang warfare on the streets of Ilford this weekend, we know it's you, and we'll come and nick you. Now, get your wife and your kids and get out of this town.'

I left the nick with my solicitor and then, once I was outside, realised that my car, which the Old Bill had towed away, was still in the nick yard, so I asked my solicitor to take me back to the nick. As I drove home, I found myself chuckling out loud – I didn't have a driving licence.

When I got back home, I loaded our bags into the car, and Laura, the kids and I set off for Maldon. As I was driving along Eastern Avenue, I noticed in my rear view mirror a dark-green car. For some reason, I felt uneasy about it. As we drove through Newbury Park towards Romford, it was still behind me.

'Laura, don't look, but there's a green car following us,' I said in a calm voice.

She looked alarmed. 'What about it?'

'It's got to be the Old Bill.'

Near Romford I pulled into a petrol station to let the dark-green car go, but it followed me in. But then, to my amazement, two nuns got out!

The caravan park was very pleasant, with lots of trees and fields, and we soon settled in. I bought a six-pack of Harp Lager from the local off-licence and sat outside the caravan taking in the country air and wondering what to do. I thought to myself, I'm in deep trouble. The Old Bill are on my case and the Romford firm are on my case. What next? While part of me was very worried, another part of me was buzzing with excitement. The armed Old Bill, the helicopter, the naughty firm, this made me feel I was on my way to making a reputation. A lot of people had heard about all of this. In a funny sort of way, I was glad it had happened.

The next morning, I went to a nearby public phone box and called my solicitor and some of the boys to see what was happening in Ilford. So far, there was nothing to report, they said.

I decided to stay at Maldon for a few days until things quietened down. The day of the meet at McDonald's came and went. I then heard from Barry the Hat that several members of the Romford firm had been nicked for a tear-up a few months earlier after a guy had been stabbed to death in a fight in a club. This was good news, I thought. The pressure was now off a little.

It was important for Laura and the kids to try and forget about what was happening and enjoy the time at Maldon, so I took them down to the town, to the river, to Colchester Zoo, and for drives around the area. It all felt quite normal in some ways.

When I returned to Ilford I discovered that the guy who Keith had cut was the nephew of this Romford firm. But with some of them now in prison, I didn't feel worried about any reprisals.

One night, I went to The Railway Tavern in Snakes Lane for a drink. A group of pikeys came in, but the landlord refused to serve them. I knew the landlord quite well, so I said, 'They're okay. They won't cause any trouble and they spend well.' I'd been working with pikeys and knew that they were okay.

He agreed to serve them. One of the pikeys then came up to me.

'Thanks for that, mate,' he said, shaking my hand.

'No problem,' I replied.

I then left The Railway Tavern and went to meet Barry the Hat in The Fir Trees in Hermon Hill, Wanstead. I was probably four times over the legal limit when I got back in my car to drive home. As I drove along Clarendon Gardens, a short distance from my flat, I skidded, lost control, and hit a big pile of sand by the side of the road. The car tipped over and spun thirty yards down the road on its roof. I can remember hearing a Grace Jones song blaring out from the cassette and then smelling petrol. Smashing the passenger window with a karate kick, I hauled myself out legs first, like a stock car driver. By this time, a group of people had gathered around the car. I staggered down the road and then ran towards home.

I told Laura what had happened and that the Old Bill would probably be round, as I had left my cheque book in the glove compartment. Sure enough, within the hour there was a loud knock at the door. I told Laura to tell them I wasn't in.

'They know you're here, Al, and they want to speak to you,' she said.

'Okay, let them in,' I said.

'Do you want to go to hospital?' asked one of the Old Bill, sitting down.

'No, I'm fine,' I answered. I knew this was a moody to take me to the nick. 'I've just had some sleeping tablets and a couple of scotches.' I said this so that they wouldn't breathalyse me.

'Well, from the state of your car, I don't know how you came out alive. When we arrived at the scene we expected to find a dead man,' said the second one.

Shortly after, I went to see Keith, who was on remand in Wandsworth prison. My mate Weasel managed to smuggle in half a bottle of whiskey in his coat pocket for him. I'd also made him some sandwiches, with speed mixed in with the butter, but had forgotten to bring them.

'Al, there's a problem,' he said when I met him in the visiting room.

'What is it?'

'You won't believe this. Two geezers from that Romford firm are in here and they're trying to give me a hard time. I ain't worried, Al, but it nearly went off the other day though.'

I advised him to contact a well-known and respected underworld figure who was banged up in Wandsworth to take the heat off. There was no way this Romford firm would tangle with him. By the time I left, he was half drunk from the whiskey, which I'd added to the numerous cups of tea I'd bought him. When I got home, I found my dog running around the flat like a lunatic.

'What's up with her, Laura?'

'Well, you know those sandwiches you made for Keith?'

'Yeah.'

She began to laugh. 'The dog's eaten them and she's off her nut.'

Keith took my advice and the situation between him and the Romford geezers was squared soon after. A few weeks later I went out with Georgie Dice and Mark, a tattooist, for a drink. We ended up outside a social club on a sprawling council estate in Romford.

As we got out of the car, Mark said, 'You know who owns this club, don't you?'

'Who?'

He mentioned the firm I'd had all the grief with.

'You're joking.' This could be naughty, I thought to myself. They might recognise me, but I wasn't going to lose face in front of my mates and not go in, that was for sure. I wanted to prove to myself that I wasn't frightened of this Romford firm.

We walked in, ordered our drinks at the bar, and sat down in the corner. Scanning the punters in the club, I felt very uneasy. I had no way of knowing if someone had clocked me. After one drink, the three of us left.

The episode with the Romford firm was not one I wanted to repeat, not because I was frightened of getting shot, but because it put my wife and kids in danger. Yet, as a result of crossing swords with this firm, I reckoned my reputation was now well and truly on the way up.

# 7

# The Showman

One Sunday afternoon in 1982 I went to a kick boxing show at the Room at the Top. It was billed as England versus Ireland and was promoted by Carl Nelson who, back then, was the only person promoting kick boxing.

It was a good show, and the fighters were very lively, but I felt it could be made more exciting. When I met some mates in The Valentine afterwards, I told them that I reckoned I could put on shows that had more razzmatazz and were more professionally run than what was currently on offer. They knew I was good at training kick boxers, but I could tell from the looks on their faces that they weren't convinced I had it in me to be a promoter. But the idea was now planted in my mind.

To bring in some extra money, Laura went to work at the nearby King Neptune fish and chip shop in Belgrave Road, which was managed by Ally the Turk. He was about thirty and a real character. Some years before, he'd been locked up in a Colombian prison after he was caught trying to set up a cocaine deal. On another occasion, he took off to America, where he acted as the promoter for Willy T, a stock car driver.

One day when I popped into his fish and chip shop, he asked me if I was interested in running an amusement arcade with him.

He told me that he'd persuaded some Turkish friends of his to let him have the lease of a grocery shop in Cranbrook Road. It sounded a good earner, so I agreed. I hired pool tables, video games and fruit machines. We rented the machines on a 60/40 split – we got 60 per cent of the takings; the owners got 40 per cent. We called the arcade 'The Corner Pocket'. However, the Old Bill closed it down after about eight months because we didn't have a licence.

With the closure of the amusement arcade, I found myself thinking more and more about staging a kick boxing show. If I'm honest, I suppose I wanted to establish myself as the guv'nor of kick boxing. I knew that the fighters who turned out for these shows never got paid. Instead, they were each presented with a plastic trophy. I figured the way to get them to fight for me was to pay them.

So I made up my mind to try my hand at putting on a show. I'd never organised anything like this before, but I felt that I knew what was needed to jazz up kick boxing. However, I needed a financial backer. But who?

I went to see my mate Georgie Dice, who was working as a printer in Waterloo and earning very good money.

'I've got this really good idea, Georgie,' I said when I met him at the bar in The Valentine.

'What is it?' he asked, lighting a Rothman.

'I want to put on a kick boxing show.'

'Kick boxing? You serious?'

'Yeah. I've been to a show and I reckon I can do it better. I can make them far more entertaining, but I need some money up front.'

We discussed the idea in more depth and, eventually, Georgie agreed to give me £1,500 to get the show up and running. He thought I was on to a winner. Excited by our new venture, we went on a real bender in the pubs and clubs in Ilford and I didn't roll in until the early hours of the morning.

When Ally the Turk came to see me I told him about my plans. In fact, Ally and I had fallen out for a while when he'd asked me to run the doors for him at a show at the Cranbrook Hall in Ilford, which he'd organised to promote his girlfriend, a brilliant soul and blues singer. I got drunk and, for some reason or other, had a row with one of his mates. But, after a while, Ally and I sorted out our differences.

'I like the sound of it, Al,' he said to me. 'I can smell pound notes. If you need any help promoting it, let me know.'

'Cheers, mate. I might need your help at some point.'

I drew up a plan. The first thing I had to do was to find some fighters, so I phoned up a number of the clubs mentioned in martial arts magazines. The first person I phoned was Chris Price, who was a Thai boxing instructor. He gave me the phone numbers of some fighters and I booked half a dozen or so of them.

Alan Davies, who was a karate instructor and who ran Stopouts wine bar in Ilford, said he would put up some of his karate fighters.

'There's a particular guy you should try and get,' he said. 'I train him and he's a terrific boxer. He fought in the Army.'

'Yeah? Okay. Have you got his number?'

He scribbled it down on a piece of paper. The guy was called Nigel Benn. I phoned him up and he invited me around to his house a few days later. After I'd explained what I was doing, he agreed to fight at the show. Little did I realise that, in 1992, this guy would become the world super middleweight champion and be known as 'The Dark Destroyer'.

I wanted to make the show something special, and so needed some sort of entertainment during the interval. But what? Then an idea came to me. I'd ask Dave Lea, a kung fu instructor I knew, to do a demonstration. Dave's party trick was to lie down between two chairs and have breeze blocks placed on his chest. One of his students would then smash them with a fourteen-pound hammer. Sometimes he'd do this lying on broken glass or a bed of nails. He'd also allow his students to place spears into his throat. Dave would tense himself up and the students would press the spears as hard as they could. Every time, the spears would bend until they broke. Another thing he did was to stand there while his students, using blow pipes, fired darts into his back.

I went to see Dave at his kung fu club in Camden Town, where he taught Hapkune-Do, a system based on the movements of the snake, tiger, dragon, crane and praying mantis. Dave was very flamboyant and had long hair. At the time, he was minder to Samantha Fox, who was a Page Three girl, and he was also a combat instructor for the US Marines in London. He later went on to become a stunt man, and was Michael Keaton's double in *Batman*.

He agreed to give a demonstration, as he saw it as a good way of promoting himself. When I told him that my sons, Sean, Adam and Jamie, were learning kick boxing, he suggested that we stage a mock contest between him and one of them. What a great idea, I thought. I would get Jamie, my second eldest, to take part. He'd love it.

I then started to think about a venue and eventually booked the Duke's Hall in Romford, which seated 300, for Friday 14 March 1986. The show would begin at 7 p.m. and there'd be seventeen fights, each consisting of three two-minute rounds, and the tickets would cost a fiver.

I decided to call myself United Karate Promotions (UKP). I designed a poster that had a black and white image of two karate fighters on it, and underneath I wrote 'Fighters from karate, kung fu and Thai boxing'. I didn't start giving shows names until later. I then went to see a printer and ordered posters, tickets and programmes.

Friends and people I knew agreed to help me run the show. Karl Nelson, Geoff Brittain and Mitch Lewis agreed to be the judges, John Day a judge/MC, and Chris Price the referee. John Hawkins's brother, Dave, would be the whip – the person who brings out the fighters. The term 'whip' in boxing dates from bare knuckle fighting when there'd be people whipping the crowd to keep them back. Steve White's wife, Christine, agreed to be the ring girl, to add a touch of glamour. Given that the show might attract its fair share of hard men and nutters, I brought in some tough guys I knew to run the door.

I needed to get some kick boxing kit for the fighters. Back then, kick boxers wore gloves that were larger than traditional boxing gloves and they were red, yellow or blue. They also wore shin pads, groin boxes, gum shields and special shoes to protect their feet. These shoes had no soles or laces. Kick boxers wore long trousers, while Thai boxers wore brightly coloured shorts that stopped just below the knee.

I did a deal with Big John, who owned Ray Jay's martial arts shop at Maryland Point. In return for allowing him to have a stall at the show, I got six sets of boxing gloves and foot pads. I then ordered a boxing ring (John Conteh once said that he could never understand why it's called the ring when, in fact, it's a square) from Fred Bentley, a boxing equipment supplier in Chelmsford, and I booked a DJ who had been recommended to me.

Once word about the show got out around east London, the tickets sold very quickly. When you are setting up any kind of business venture for the first time, you can never be absolutely sure that you will make the sales you expect. The icing on the cake was when Georgie obtained a drinks licence for the evening, so we could run our own bar.

When other promoters heard about what I was planning to do they weren't too happy. Phil Mayo phoned me up and asked if I wanted to join the Contact Karate Organisation (CKO), which he ran. I told him, thanks, but no thanks – I wanted to do my own thing. I could tell he wasn't pleased.

On the afternoon of the fight Georgie and I, dressed in evening suits and dickie bows, went to a local off-licence and loaded up his estate car with booze. It was a wonder we were able to get the car moving as we had so much stuff in it. I felt a mixture of excitement and nervousness as we drove over to Romford. All my hard work over the last four months was about to come to fruition. But I was worried that something might go wrong. Would all the fighters turn up? Would the friends who'd offered to help turn up? Had I organised the evening well enough? In terms of the actual fights, I was particularly looking forward to Nigel Benn's bout with Pat

O'Keefe, a very experienced kick boxer. Would Nigel be as good as people said he was? I'd know in a few hours.

When we arrived at the hall, I was relieved to see Fred Bentley putting the finishing touches to the boxing ring. I then got a phone call from the DJ to say that he'd broken down near Dartford in Kent. When Ray Ellis, a mate, heard this he agreed to go and pick him up.

By 7 p.m. the hall was packed. There must have been 700 punters rammed in, some of them very tough-looking characters, and many suited and booted and accompanied by their girlfriends. Georgie and I pushed our way through the crowds and climbed under the ropes into the ring, gave a triumphant wave to the cheering crowd, and then returned to our front row seats. When John Day announced the first fight, roars went up from the audience. As the first two fighters emerged into the hall, to 'The Eye of the Tiger', the theme music from *Rocky*, the atmosphere was electric.

Eventually, it was Nigel Benn's turn to fight. Watching him get into the ring, with a fiercely determined expression, I thought he looked like a lion about to go after its prey. He turned out to be awesome, and produced some incredible punches along with spinning kicks and jumping spinning kicks. Pat O'Keefe held him off for a while, but in the end he couldn't stand up to Nigel's lethal punches and kicks. One particularly vicious kick broke his arm.

In the interval Dave Lea did one of his demonstrations with some of his students. Afterwards, he took the mike and said, 'There's someone in this hall who wants to challenge me.'

Murmurs rippled around the hall. You could tell that people were thinking, 'Who'd be stupid enough to fight this bloke?'

'Come on! Where are you?' bellowed Dave, leaning over the ropes.

Then up stepped the challenger: my seven-year-old son Jamie, dressed in a grey tracksuit and wearing huge boxing gloves. Huge cheers went up from the crowd as he was hoisted into the ring.

Watching him go through his moves with Dave, I felt so proud. Dave was great, and made out that Jamie was too good for him by falling over a couple of times and making grimacing expressions, as if Jamie had hurt him. At the end, he let Jamie hit him on the chin and pretended to be knocked out. Both Dave and Jamie got a standing ovation from the crowd.

The week before the fight, I'd read a story in the *Ilford Recorder* about a pensioner called Herbert Eustace, who'd been robbed and viciously beaten up. I was appalled by this and contacted the paper and told them we'd hold a collection for the man at the show. I placed enlarged photos of him in the foyer and put a poster up saying that we'd be collecting for him during the interval. So, after Dave's demonstration, buckets were passed around the crowd and we raised two hundred and fifty quid.

After clearing up and paying the fighters (I was the first promoter to pay Nigel Benn for a fight), we drove to Georgie's house, where we counted the money and got the drinks out. I drank and drank. The night had been a massive success and we were buzzing. We had made about three grand on the bar.

'I'll tell you what, Georgie,' I said, still replaying the night in my mind.

'What, Al?'

'The next one's going to be even bigger.'

My next show was in June at Ilford Town Hall. It went even better than Romford and over 800 punters turned up. In the interval, with music from Frankie Goes to Hollywood blaring over the speakers, Jamie, along with Terry Buttwell's eight-year-old son, wearing protective head gear, did a kick boxing demonstration of three one-minute rounds. But this proved to be controversial. Interviewed on Thames TV, a leading neurologist said he was appalled at children taking up kick boxing, and he went on to claim that it was more dangerous than traditional boxing. When they interviewed me, I pointed out that the boys were in protective gear and that they were probably more at risk in the school playground.

At the age of thirty, I passed my driving test, and then took Laura and the boys for a well-earned holiday to the Costa del Sol in Spain. By now, I was regularly smoking dope at night to chill out.

Our fourth son, Mel, had been born on 23 September 1986, at Whipps Cross Hospital. Ally the Turk came to the hospital to take some photos of him, and then put them in an album which he presented to Laura and me. Inside, he wrote, 'Welcome to the world. Be strong. May you grow to be a fighter.'

In October, I staged my third show, at York Hall, Bethnal Green, in front of 1,000 punters. After this, there was a real buzz on the circuit, and people wanted to know who this bloke Alan Mortlock was. I was now making a name for myself on the kick boxing circuit.

The promoting was really taking off and I began to look for fighters from around Britain. I felt I was on a roll as every show I did seemed better than the last one. In order to look the part, I took to wearing a shirt and tie and smart suits instead of tracksuits or jeans.

One newspaper wrote that kick boxing could become more popular than wrestling, which was still big in Britain in the mid-1980s. Nigel Benn fought again for me, at York Hall, against Steve Cross, who was two stone heavier than him. Nigel knocked him out in the second round, and soon after that he went professional.

In order to bring in some extra money, I then opened a kick boxing club in a upstairs room at Cathall Road Leisure Centre with Terry Buttwell, who'd fought on the bill at Duke's Hall. As I had seventeen years' experience in martial arts and fighting, I felt confident that I had the knowledge and ability to train fighters.

Not long after, I attended my first unlicensed boxing show, at Walthamstow Football Club. Charlie Smith, the promoter, asked me if I'd arrange for a couple of kick boxers to go on the bill. He said he'd pay me one hundred quid. I'll always remember it because halfway through the show someone let off CS gas and fighting broke out in the audience.

I was out drinking in The Bald Hind in Chigwell one Bank

Holiday Monday with Georgie and Johnny the Doorman, who worked at the Villa night club across the road, and Weasel. Weasel, who was six foot seven, seventeen stone, and had a piercing stare, was also a doorman. After a bloke was stabbed to death during a massive fight at a club in Essex one night, he had been charged with murder. But when the case went to the Old Bailey, his barrister argued that he'd killed the man in self-defence, and he was acquitted.

'I want to sort out some pikeys. They've been causing problems at the club. Will you all give me a hand?' said Johnny.

'Why, what have they been up to, man?' I asked.

'Giving me a lot of grief,' he replied.

The three of us said we'd give him a hand. We then drove in Weasel's Ford Granada to The White Hart pub in Woodford Bridge for another drink. As we walked in, and I don't know why, I jumped in the air and did a jumping spinning kick, with the result that I split the hat stand in two.

'I've only ever seen that done in a kung fu movie,' laughed Georgie.

We stood at the bar and waited to get served.

'You're not drinking in my pub,' said the guv'nor, walking over to us.

'Why not?' asked Johnny.

'It's obvious why not. Look what your mate has done to my hat stand.'

We couldn't be bothered to argue, and we weren't bullies, so we left and then drove to The Railway Tavern, where we expected the pikeys to be. We walked through the doors to find that it was full of pikeys of all ages.

'I'm off,' said Georgie. 'You can't take this lot on.'

'Course we can,' said Johnny.

'You must be mad,' retorted Georgie, and he quickly walked straight back out.

The next minute, a stocky, bearded gypsy came over to us and stood there provocatively, with his hand gripping an empty pint glass. 'I'm going to stick this in your face,' he snarled. With that, I heard chairs scraping as everyone in the pub stood up.

'Come on, then,' I challenged.

'That's enough! That's enough!' bellowed someone from the other bar. An older man with an authoritative manner then appeared. He looked vaguely familiar, I thought to myself.

He came up to where the bearded pikey and I were standing and stood between us. 'Apologise!' he shouted angrily at the pikey who'd threatened me.

'I'm sorry,' he muttered, looking at the floor.

'Now, buy him a drink,' ordered the older man, giving me a friendly nod. 'This man helped us out last year when the guv'nor wouldn't serve us.'

Then the penny dropped. This was the leader of the pikeys, and he was repaying me for persuading the previous landlord of The Railway Tavern not to ban the pikeys.

As we left the pub, an Old Bill car pulled up outside. They stopped me and asked what was going on. I replied, 'Nothing', and we chirpily bid them good night and got into Weasel's Granada. I clambered into the passenger seat and Johnny got into the back. Weasel then sped off with his foot on the accelerator. The speedometer shot up to 60 mph. Weasel and I began singing 'There's no business like show business', but Johnny sat there quietly. He looked petrified. Suddenly hearing him open the door handle, I turned around to see the door open and Johnny rolling along the road, like someone out of a cartoon. I closed the door and Weasel and I carried on towards Ilford.

The next thing I can remember was the car spinning out of control, a big thud, and then fumbling for the door. I staggered out and Weasel did the same. We stood there, dazed and not knowing what to say to each other, both of us looking at the car, which had turned upside down. The wheels were still spinning around. And then Weasel, for some reason, pressed the electronic key fob to activate the alarm. We flagged down a passing car and we were given a lift back to Ilford. To this day, I don't know how we got out of that car alive. I didn't see Johnny for ages after that, so I never did find out exactly why he jumped, or whether he got away without injuring himself.

But that was not the only time I was involved in crazy driving. One summer night John Hawkins and I went out in my gold Mercedes to a few pubs. We'd been drinking all day at the house of an ex-boxer in Woodford Green, where we'd been doing some plastering. It was a pretty uneventful night, as we had just had a few pints, played a few games of pool, and chatted with some mates.

When we were driving back to Ilford I spotted what I thought was an unmarked Old Bill car following us.

'John, the Old Bill are behind.'

'How do you know?'

'I can tell. They often drive dark-red Cavaliers.'

'Are you sure, Al?' he asked, looking behind him.

'Yeah,' I answered, slamming my foot on the accelerator.

I headed for Georgie Dice's house in Gants Hill as I knew I could hide the Merc in his garage. I tried to lose the Old Bill by cutting through the back streets. As I screeched around corners, I collided with several parked cars.

Suddenly I found myself approaching Eastern Avenue, a busy dual carriageway. I slowed down, pushed the door and jumped out, leaving a petrified John still in the car, and then legged it along the dual carriageway towards Georgie's house.

I could hear the voices of Old Bill shouting and swearing at me to stop. I ran down an alleyway and jumped over a wall, into a back garden. Crouching there, trying to get my breath back, I could hear the sound of the Old Bill boots crunching along the alleyway. I then noticed that the door to the garage was open, so I slithered on my stomach across the grass towards it. Once inside, I pulled the door shut and waited, my heart pounding.

The next minute, the door burst open and an alsatian dog leapt through the air towards me. I put my hands up to protect myself, but the dog began biting my left thigh. I tried to shake it off, but it refused to let go, so I did an axe kick on its head. It let go of my thigh and then started biting my calf. I then began punching and kicking and got hold of it around its neck and ears. It didn't let go until an Old Bill pulled it off.

I was arrested and taken to Ilford nick. I was worried that I might be sent down again, as I had some amphetamine sulphate in my pocket. So when I was booked in, I threw it down on the counter. I was then banged up in a cell.

After protesting about my injuries from the alsatian dog, the Old Bill doctor examined me and said, as I expected, that I was okay. But I felt awful; I had bruises and teeth marks on my thighs where the dog had bitten me. I complained to my solicitor that the Old Bill had left me alone with the dog for an excessive time, and in the end he did a deal with the Old Bill. I was charged with being under the influence of drink or drugs.

When the case went to Redbridge Magistrates Court, to my huge relief, I just ended up with a three-year driving ban and a two hundred quid fine, rather than a prison sentence.

I was still doing some building work during this period, and at one job in Clerkenwell I found myself working with a bricklayer called Johnny. It turned out he was the brother of Micky Mannion, who I used to spar with in Camp Hill. Another guy working with us was Gerry O'Dowd, who was Boy George's brother. I once went with them and Ally the Turk to Slim Jim's gym in Greenwich, south-east London, where I was introduced to Lenny McLean, the legendary bare knuckle fighter and unlicensed boxer. Lenny had an incredibly powerful punch. While I was in the gym, I watched him smash his fist into the punch bag, sending both it and the bloke who was holding it flying through the air.

I was sitting at home one day in 1987 when Jack Boas, a Dutch kick boxing trainer who was living in Lincoln, asked if I'd be interested in him bringing a team of Dutch fighters over for a Thai boxing and kick boxing show I was in the process of promoting. At the time, Thai boxing was very big in Holland. Some shows were attracting crowds of 2,000. I immediately agreed to work with Jack and his contacts in Amsterdam.

We held the show at York Hall. We had two women on the bill; Kelly Berry from south London and Dangerous Dagma from Holland. Kelly was good, but Dangerous Dagma knocked her out in the second round. Women kick boxers can fight just as hard as men, and the punters love to watch them. During the show, one of the crowd picked up the spit bucket and threw it into the ring, hitting Jack with it.

One night when I was acting as a judge for Phil Mayo at a kick boxing show at the Poplar Civic Centre, I met an American kick boxing promoter called Mike Sawyer, who ran the International Sport Karate Association. We swapped phone numbers and said we'd stay in touch.

A couple of months later, he contacted me and invited me to bring a team of fighters over to Daytona Beach, Florida. I took five fighters over there, and the show took place at an 11,000-seater stadium; it was a great success. What was amusing was that one of my fighters, Derek Idon, who was nicknamed 'The Iron Man', had a fear of flying. It took me ages to persuade him to fly out to Florida. On the return flight, the plane ran into serious turbulence and began violently shaking. Passengers were screaming and we all thought we were going to crash, but, thankfully, we landed safely.

Terry Buttwell and I split and we pulled out of Cathall Road Leisure Centre, and I opened my own kick boxing club, the Stable Gym, in a room at the back of a café in Manor Road, Woodford Bridge, and Terry opened the Bulldog Gym in Cathall Road.

I occasionally worked the doors in a West End night club and helped sort out trouble in a few pubs. I'd sit in pubs all night with another guy looking out for known troublemakers. I used to carry an ammonia squirt in my jacket pocket, while the other guy carried a spring-loaded cosh.

Laura and I moved from Seymour Gardens to a three-bedroom Victorian semi in a street off High Road, Leyton, about three miles away. I was now training at the same gym as Nigel Benn, which was above The Central pub in East Ham. Nigel had become

Commonwealth middleweight champion by now and was coming up to fight Michael Watson.

One day I said to him, 'Would you be prepared to put the name of a karate manufacturer on your gown when you fight?'

'Yes, okay, Al,' he said.

'How much will you want?'

'Just get me some punch bags and gloves,' he replied.

Ally the Turk and I went to Kwon, a karate equipment manufacturer, and asked them if they would sponsor our fights if we got their name and logo, a fist, on the back of Nigel Benn's gown on his next televised fight, which was at Glasgow's Kelvin Hall. They agreed. When the fight was shown they were over the moon to see their company's name on TV.

I also went to see Charlie Magri, the former world flyweight champion, who had a sports shop in Bethnal Green Road, and I got him to agree to putting his photo on a poster for a fight.

Through my kick boxing shows I'd become friendly with Es Kaitell, a six foot six black guy who ran a car valet service and a security company, which supplied door staff to pubs and clubs. Es had a real reputation. He asked me to go with him and another guy to sort out a spot of bother he was having with a mini-cab company in Romford. When I got into the car, he handed me something wrapped in a cloth.

'Hang on to this, Al,' he said.

I took it from him and saw that it was a gun. 'Are you going to use that?' I asked, thinking I didn't really want to get caught up in a shooting.

'I hope I don't have to,' he replied. 'But I'm going prepared, man.'

When we arrived at the cab office, near Hollywood Boulevard night club, he told me and the other guy to wait outside and he disappeared into the office. I could hear raised voices inside; I sat there, expecting to hear shots at any minute. He emerged a few minutes later.

'Sorted?' I asked.

He smiled back. 'Sorted.'

I was asked if I'd promote a charity boxing contest at Poplar Civic Centre. The idea was that non-trained guys from the Poplar, Plaistow, Canning Town and Stratford areas would fight each other and the money raised would go to a woman who had cancer. Money would also be raised by selling paintings by Reggie and Ronnie Kray, and Harry Roberts, in the Lord Raglan in Plaistow.

This was when I met Mickey Peterson – better known today as Charles Bronson, and regarded as one of the most violent men in the country – it's said that he once fought a Rottweiler dog and killed it. He'd just come out of Broadmoor. A big, powerfully built bloke with short cropped hair and a thick moustache and neatly trimmed beard, he reminded me of someone from the French Foreign Legion.

In the changing room I helped him warm up for the fight. In other words, I put pads on my hands and he punched them. He was a strong puncher – I know this because one of his jabs missed the pad and caught me on the chin.

When it came to his fight, he went berserk and punched like a machine. The other bloke didn't stand a chance and was soon flat on his back. But Mickey carried on pounding him mercilessly, and three of us had to jump on him and pull him off.

At the end of the evening I went to the Crews Club at Fairlop Waters leisure complex for a celebratory booze-up. As a thank you, the organisers presented me with a cake in the shape of a boxing ring.

Another time, I put on a Thai kick boxing show in a West End hotel. After the show, a well-spoken man came up to me and introduced himself as Keith Sewell, a film producer. He told me he'd like to make a film about kick boxing, so we swapped cards, and I thought no more about it. Out of the blue, a few weeks later, he phoned me up to say that he had a financial backer for a film. He said that he wanted me to put on the biggest-ever kick boxing show and film it as a one-hour drama documentary. He told me that some rich guy in Hadleigh Wood, Essex, who had made his money selling mobile phones, which were then just taking off, was prepared to back the film. It sounded brilliant, and there'd be a nice few quid in it.

So the following week, I went over to this big house in Hadleigh Wood with Ally the Turk, and took with us some video tapes and posters of the shows. The film producer introduced us to Paul, a quietly spoken man, and Ian, his associate, who I immediately took a dislike to. He was trying to act the hard man, and I knew it was all front.

After watching the videos, Paul was very enthusiastic. The producer explained that he planned to use John Conteh and the actor Michael Elphick as narrators for the film, which would be called *Just for Kicks*. I was impressed.

We then went back to my house and discussed the show, how much it would cost to stage, and how much we would expect to get paid. Finally, we went back to them and hammered out an agreement. Ally managed to negotiate me a very good promoters' fee of about eight grand.

The show was fixed for Saturday 22 April 1989, at the Great Hall, Pickets Lock Centre, Edmonton, a 2,000-seater venue that we easily expected to fill, because this would be a show like no other. It would be presented as England versus the USA versus Holland.

I rented secretarial services from the company that owned the building in Harrow Road where Ally had an office, and I changed my name to United Kick Boxing Promotions.

I knew that I couldn't afford to mess up with the show, so I virtually stopped drinking. I'd have an occasional pint, but in no way would I allow myself to go on benders. I had to have a clear head to plan the event, and although this was very hard, I was determined to make this show a massive success. There was no telling where it might lead.

I contacted Mike Sawyer, the Florida boxing promoter, and asked him if he'd bring some fighters over for the show. He thought this was a great idea and, after we agreed a fee, he said he'd bring over some of his best ones.

Nigel Benn agreed to make a guest appearance at the show, along with world kick boxing champion Ronnie Green. This was flagged up on the posters, which were printed in red, blue and white and carried the flags of each country.

Because I wanted the American fighters to arrive in style, I booked stretch limousines to pick them up from Gatwick Airport and take them to their hotel. I'd assumed they would be in and out of stretch limos all the time, as they were Americans – but they told me that they were country boys and had never been in one in their lives. Two of the Dutch fighters were called The Brothers Crimm. Inevitably, I nicknamed them The Brothers Grimm.

I was excited when Ally and I arrived at the Pickets Lock Centre on the afternoon of the fight. The place was buzzing with activity. There were the film crew, electricians, carpenters, labourers and staff from the centre scurrying around everywhere. Two men were draping flags from the ceiling, other blokes were putting the ring up, and there were cables and lights everywhere. Looking around at the 2,000 empty seats, I thought to myself, 'This is going to be some night.'

'Well, it's all taking shape,' I said cheerily to Keith.

He frowned. 'We've got a big problem.'

'What?'

'We don't have the tower for the cameras. The guy who should have ordered it forgot.'

'Well, I know a mate who can supply scaffolding,' I said, thinking quickly. 'Tell me what you need.'

He brightened up at this. 'Brilliant.'

I phoned a mate who ran a building firm, and two hours later a lorry full of scaffolding arrived. His men worked quickly and soon they had erected a thirty-foot tower.

I had a lot of jobs to do before the fight started, such as check-ing that the fighters knew the running order and rules, briefing Es Kaitell's security team, meeting the VIPs, and going on the pads with Growling Glen Wild, who I'd trained, and was on the bill.

The first punters started arriving at about 6 p.m. and by 6.45 the hall was nearly full. As the fighters came out, rave music blared out. The MC, a professional entertainer, was dressed in full Uncle Sam regalia. In the interval, Dave Lea brought in a team of Chinese martial arts experts. They were all inside a lion costume and they danced around the ring, banging drums (I later discovered that they were Triads). It all went to plan – except when one of the fighters fell out of the ring and landed on Nigel Benn, who shoved him back through the ropes.

After the show, we went to a party at The General Havelock pub in Havelock Street, Ilford. I was still on a high and the champagne and the coke flowed all night.

Funnily enough, the film they made was never transmitted, but it had led to a great show being put on and had been an invaluable experience. I felt good about myself and the money was coming in. I felt that I'd arrived. I was no longer Alan Mortlock, the ducker and diver. I was a top kick boxing promoter.

Putting her arms around me, Laura said, 'Al, this is our passport to better things.'

I sipped a glass of champagne. 'I know, love. Life is going to be good.'

How wrong I was.

# 8

# Hitting the Bottle

I was sitting at the bar of The Birbeck Tavern in Langthorne Road, Leytonstone, one night. It had become a dive of a pub, and I'd once remarked to Laura, 'I don't know how anyone can drink in there. It's filthy.'

I looked up to see Laura standing there, glaring fiercely at me. 'Want a drink, love?' I slurred, and signalled to Martin, the guv'nor, who was pouring himself a whiskey.

She scowled at me, then, without warning, snatched the drink from my hand and threw it in my face.

'What you doing?' I exclaimed, jumping up off my stool.

'You're out drinking every day. And I'm sick of it!' she screamed.

''Ere, 'ere. That's enough,' said Martin sternly, moving to the bar. He was quite drunk as well. 'He's okay.'

'Are you coming home?' she demanded, ignoring his protests. The fact that Martin was also drunk seemed to make her more angry.

'No. I'm not,' I replied, drying my head with a bar towel and becoming aware that all the customers had their eyes turned towards me. 'Give me another pint, Martin.'

'No! Come home,' Laura shouted at me.

'I've told you that's enough. Now, out you go,' said Martin sharply.

The next minute, Laura grabbed a glass off the bar and hurled it at him. It missed and smashed into the bottles of spirits. With that, she stormed out of the pub.

The Pickets Lock show had really put me on the map. One magazine described me as 'The Frank Warren of kick boxing'. I was getting loads of phone calls from trainers, fighters and punters congratulating me on putting on such a fantastic event. Everyone felt that I was taking kick boxing forward to a new level. Looking back, this should have been one of the best periods of my life, but instead it turned out to be one of the worst.

I'd always been a big drinker but, without realising it, I was spending more and more time in the pub, and my work as a kick boxing promoter soon started to dry up. Due to the booze, the hangovers and the speed and coke I snorted, I began to lose the plot. Because I didn't have a clear mind, I'd avoid answering the phone. When anyone in a pub asked me how the kick boxing was going, I'd usually make out that I was planning to put another show on in the near future. But nothing was further from my mind.

When I walked through the doors of a pub and ordered a pint, I would want another, and then another. I couldn't stop at just a couple. Whereas at one time I drank Foster's, I was now drinking the strong lagers, such as Tennants Extra, Lowenbrau and Stella. It was common for me to drink as many as twenty-five pints a day, five days a week. I just drank and drank, with no thought for the next day.

And my approach to pubs changed. When I lived in Seymour Gardens, I'd go to The Valentine, then probably to Stopouts wine bar, and then on to the Villa night club. But now the drink had become more important than where I drank. I just floated around between The King Harold, which was just down the road from Leyton tube station, and where geezers on mobile phones hung around at night to sell drugs, Wheelers on Leyton Road and The Birbeck Tavern. Martin, the guv'nor at The Birbeck, was an alcoholic and he'd frequently fall over behind the bar. If this happened, we'd all lean over and help ourselves to free drinks from the pumps.

Boozers always gravitate towards other boozers, and I was now boozing with hardened drinkers, such as Little Ronnie and Pat. These blokes weren't duckers and divers or out for a tear-up. They worked hard, and nearly all of them were divorced or on their way to getting divorced – usually because of the drink. We became more drinking partners than mates.

I was in the pub every day, morning and night, and hardly spent any time at home. As a result, my marriage began to collapse and I was becoming distant from my four kids. Adam was now thirteen, Jamie, eleven, Sean, ten, and Mel, three.

John Hawkins and I had landed a very well-paid sub-contract renovating Salvation Army buildings. We did pointing, plastering, underpinning and rendering. I remember the time we were doing a job in Ware, Hertfordshire. Each lunchtime we went to a local pub for a few pints, but after that we were never in a fit state to work. One day, we went back to the building site after a drink in the pub, where John had been slinging back double whiskeys. I was pointing the wall and John was working on the guttering. I watched concerned as John stood a double extension aluminium ladder on a metal box. When I told him that to put metal against metal was dangerous, he laughed and said it was okay. He climbed up the ladder and then, all of a sudden, it gave way and he fell twenty-five feet, landing on the ground with a thud. He was in agony. When the labourer who was working with us asked me what we should do, I just told him to mix some more cement. I was more annoyed with John for being so stupid than concerned about him. Eventually, though, I helped him into the back of my car and drove straight to the casualty department of Whipps Cross Hospital.

Soon after that, we lost the contract after failing to turn up at a job in St Albans. The day before we were due to start the job was my birthday. That night, John and I went out for a big booze-up at The Chestnut Tree in Lea Bridge Road. We stayed in the pub all night with the guv'nor, drinking and sniffing speed. I didn't arrive home until 9.30 a.m. Still drunk, I went straight to bed. The next day, the main contractor told me that there was no more work for us. I felt gutted, especially as Christmas was a few weeks away.

As Laura and I were now short of money, I resorted to signing on at the DHSS. I just couldn't seem to get myself back on the rails.

When I was drinking in The King Harold one afternoon, my son Adam turned up and told me that Laura had had her handbag nicked when she was in the Co-op in Leytonstone. I left my drink and headed home with him. On the way, in High Road, Leyton, a man came up to me and handed me something. I looked at it and saw that it was a leaflet about the Bible. I smiled politely, took it from him, and absentmindedly stuffed it in the inside pocket of my jacket. Christianity was the last thing I needed in my life. I needed money.

There were times when I'd disappear from home for three days, spending the nights sleeping in the houses of other boozers I knew, and wearing the same clothes for days on end. I'd wake up in the morning, nursing a terrible hangover, feeling disgusted with myself, and thinking, I want to go home. But then the guilt would kick in and I'd head, bleary-eyed, off to a pub for another drink. After two or three lagers I'd be able to block these feelings out, and I'd be off on another bender.

I remember waking up one morning on the settee in some bloke's flat and seeing an image of Laura and Mel, my youngest boy, in my mind. The guilt was crippling. It was so bad that I got butterflies in my stomach. In order to forget about the pain, I forced myself back to sleep.

Laura and I began rowing at home. One time, I came home after drinking solidly for two days and I got into a blazing row with her. Suddenly, in anger, I took a flying kick at the door and smashed a hole in it.

I'd always been violent, but now I found myself flying off the handle for no reason at all. One night I was in Wheelers, chatting with a few guys at the bar. One of them thought that he might be able to get me some plastering work. I'd been on the beer since the morning and things were, by now, starting to become a bit blurred. My mate Gary, who was about ten years younger than me, then walked in.

'Okay, Al,' he said jovially, patting me on the back. I spun around. 'Don't do that!' I snapped.

'What?'

'Hit me on the back like that,' I said angrily.

'Leave it out, Al. I'm only being friendly,' Gary grinned, looking at his mates.

I put my drink down on the bar and faced him. 'I said don't do it. Got it?'

He shrugged his shoulders and began to make his way over to the pool table.

I went after him and tried to get hold of him around the neck, but the strength had gone out of me, as I'd been drinking for two days and could hardly stand up. We struggled with each other and ended up outside. Gary then head-butted me, slightly cutting my right eye, and I staggered back. He grabbed hold of me to restrain me. Eventually, he let me go, and the two of us went back into the pub, and I carried on drinking.

The next morning, Gary phoned me up. 'Al, mate, I'm sorry about last night. Honestly. I didn't mean it.' There was fear in his voice.

'Listen,' I replied. 'Don't worry about it – I've learnt my lesson. I should stop this drinking.' But I knew as soon as I said the words that I wouldn't stop. I'd said this so many times before.

Sometimes I'd go into a pub and the landlord would refuse to serve me because I had caused trouble the night before, and I wouldn't have a clue what he was talking about. I remember I was once in the Blackbirds, just down the road from The King Harold and opposite a car showroom that was owned by a mate of mine. I'd been on a three-day bender and must have drunk a hundred pints during that time. When I left the pub, I sat on the brick wall outside and then fell over. I broke several ribs and had to go to Whipps Cross Hospital.

Laura was unable to sleep and was constantly in tears. In retro-spect, she was probably close to a nervous breakdown.

When I used to lie in bed at night, when I hadn't been out drinking, I'd look at Laura and the kids and think, 'Why am I doing this?' And I'd hear a voice saying, 'Eff them. You don't need them.' Sometimes I'd be in a boozer and I'd see Adam, my eldest son, sitting on his push-bike looking wonderingly at me through the window. I'd wave back cheerily and then, feeling ashamed and selfish, turn away and take a swig from my pint.

I remember once being in The Thatched House in High Road, Leytonstone, a pub where I didn't know anyone. I was half-drunk by the time I walked in, as I'd been drinking solid for nearly four days. There was a group of black guys there, standing around the bar or playing pool. As I ordered a drink, one of them came over to me.

'Hi, Al.'

'Do I know you?' I asked, trying to focus on him.

'Yeah. I've met you at The Valentine and you've sold me some gear.'

'Oh yeah,' I said, taking a sip of my pint.

He smiled at me. 'Listen, man. Are you interested in making some money?'

'Some money?'

'Yeah. If you can get three hundred quid together we can make a lot of money selling crack.'

'Oh yeah,' I muttered, draining my pint and signalling to the barmaid for another. I was only going through the motions of listening. I didn't really know what crack was.

'Crack's selling for a fortune on the streets. It gives you a real buzz, man. And there's a lot of people out there who will pay good money for it,' he continued.

I shook my head, unable to take on board what he was saying. 'Sorry, mate.' I returned to my pint and carried on drinking.

One night I was on my travels in Ilford, going from pub to pub, when I met Rob in The Valentine. Like me, he was a boozer and a ducker and diver.

'Have you heard about Steve White?' he asked.

'No. What's he done?' I'd not seen Steve for about eighteen months, and I was wondering where he'd got to.

'He's been nicked, and he's looking at a six. But listen to this,' continued Rob, with incredulity in his voice. 'He's got religion.'

'You what?'

'Straight up. They reckon he's become a Christian.'

'Come off it! Steve, a Christian?' I burst into laughter. Apart from the drug dealing, Steve had been done for all sorts of other stuff, including kidnapping, fraud, demanding money with menaces and blackmail.

That night, I phoned Steve to find out why he'd been nicked. Straightaway he started talking about Jesus, and I told him to stop talking rubbish and then put the phone down. I thought to myself, I know his game, he's just using this Christianity lark to try and reduce his sentence. In the past, Steve had been charged with a number of drug-related offences and had done time in prison.

Another day, I was drinking with John Hawkins in Walthamstow. We came out of The Nag's Head in the middle of the afternoon and staggered through a graveyard next to an old church, not really sure where we were going. I don't know why, but anger suddenly welled up inside of me and I began looking up at the sky and shouting at God. Why was I doing this? I didn't believe in God.

'Can you hear me?' I cried, shaking my fist in the air. 'Are you up there? If you are, show me.'

'What you on about, Al?' asked John, laughing.

'I don't know, John,' I muttered.

'Come on, Al, let's get another drink,' he said, placing his hand on my arm. We found another pub and carried on drinking.

When I woke up in the morning, hung over as usual and only able to think about going to the pub again, I had a strange feeling. I began to think about that incident in the churchyard and felt I'd overstepped the mark in some way. An uneasiness and fear went through me, but I didn't know why. I mean, I didn't believe in God.

So why did I feel this way?

I told Laura what I'd done in the churchyard. 'You are always up to something or other,' she smiled thinly, shaking her head.

One Saturday night I was in the King Harold with Jimmy. We'd started off drinking there that morning and then gone to Woodford for a session. Jimmy was a nutter. One of his party tricks was to grab hold of someone by the windpipe and squeeze them until they fainted. In fact, two weeks before the guv'nor of The King Harold had phoned me one Friday night and asked me to go down there to watch his back, as Jimmy looked like he might cause trouble. The guv'nor gave me fifty quid for this.

We then got into an argument with Alex, the guv'nor of The Oliver Twist, and his mate, John, a doorman who was a massive bloke. I can't even recall what it was about.

'Come on then,' taunted Jimmy. 'Do you want some?'

Alex, who was a boxer, immediately lashed out at Jimmy, catching him on the chin. In a flash, Jimmy whipped out a screwdriver and stabbed Alex across the cheek. He collapsed on to the bar, screaming and clutching his face. I then steamed into John and the two of us ended up brawling outside.

On Sunday lunchtime, I returned to The King Harold. 'Al, they're going to come after you,' said the guv'nor with a worried look.

'What do you mean?'

'Alex. He's after you and he's brought a load of pikeys from all over London. They're all down The Oliver Twist.'

'Yeah,' I answered casually.

'Look, let me try and sort it out.'

'I'll deal with it,' I said cockily. I knew what I had to do: go round to The Oliver Twist and face Alex.

When I got there I rang the bell. The Oliver Twist was in Oliver Road, and it was often closed, but there'd still be people drinking inside. I waited with a mixture of apprehension and a sort of excitement running through me. Someone opened the door and I walked in. I couldn't believe it – it was packed with hard-looking pikeys. What had I let myself in for? I thought, looking around me. They all went quiet and stared at me. I stood there for a moment, wondering what to do, then turned around and walked back out.

But halfway up the road my pride kicked in. I'd lost my bottle. Then I remembered the fight with Gary; I was frightened, not of the pikeys, but of losing my reputation. Right, I thought, I'll show them I'm not scared, so I went back to the pub, rang the bell again, walked in, and strode confidently through the middle of the pikeys and straight up to Alex. I felt as if I were walking through a gauntlet.

We stood facing each other and the pub went quiet. Any minute now it's going to go off, I thought. In my mind, I could picture glasses and chairs flying through the air and me being bang in trouble.

'Okay, how do you want to be?' I said in a business-like manner, looking him in the eye.

He knew what I meant. Hesitating, he moved towards me, then, to my surprise, stopped and said, 'All respect to you. You've come in here on your own.' He held out his hand.

Well, this was a turn up, I thought.

'Yeah, I can't believe you've had the bottle to come in here on your own and stand your ground,' said another pikey.

Alex then bought me a pint and I spent the rest of the day drinking in the pub.

As Christmas approached, things were going from bad to worse at home. We had no money to buy presents, as I hadn't had an earner since the last kick boxing show, and I hadn't had a major building job for ages.

Laura and I were becoming more and more like enemies, and increasingly distant from each other. I used to constantly say to her the morning after a bender, 'I'm never going to drink again.' But, of course, I always did.

I came downstairs one morning, rubbing the sleep from my eyes and feeling awful, and went into the kitchen, where Laura was ironing the kids' clothes. There was a stony silence between us. I made myself a cup of tea and tried to get myself back into the land of the living.

'Alan. Can I say something?'

'What?'

'Do you realise that you haven't eaten once at home this month?'

'Yeah,' I replied, taking a sip from my tea and turning towards the living room.

'You come back every night drunk – when you do come back,' she said bitterly. 'Some nights you literally fall through the door. I don't know how you make it home. You have to cross busy roads. It's a wonder that you haven't been knocked down by now.'

'Well, I do make it home, don't I,' I snapped back.

She paused and put down the iron. 'Alan, I don't know how much more of this I can take. I stuck by you when you were in prison and I've stuck by you through all your fighting. I do love you, but I can't go on living like this. You're not the man I married any more.'

I grunted and tried to ignore what she was saying.

'What's happened to you?' she continued. 'Your boxing promoting was going so well. You were really making a name for yourself. Remember how fantastic that show was at Pickets Lock and how we saw it as the passport to a good life. But now look at you. You've thrown it all away.'

I sat there in silence, not knowing what to say. She was right – we'd been married for seventeen years. At one time, we'd been madly in love. What had happened? How had it all gone so wrong?

She looked down at the floor and then said with sadness, 'I've had enough. I really can't carry on like this any more. I've told the children that we're going to get a divorce. But let's get Christmas out of the way first.'

'Fine,' I replied nonchalantly, not really taking in her words. It was too early in the morning to get into an argument, so I took my tea into the living room and wondered what the day would bring.

My kids were distraught at the thought of us breaking up. A few days later, one of the teachers at Sean's school phoned to say that he was crying a lot, for no reason. She wanted to know what the problem was. And Adam, my oldest son, started blaming Laura for the fact that we were going to get divorced. One day, he turned around to her angrily and said, 'This is all your fault. Why don't you leave him alone.'

I remember going with Laura and Mel to see *Sleeping Beauty* at the Plaza cinema in South Woodford. Sitting there seeing all those families, the happiness in the film, hearing the music, and thinking about the time of the year, was all too much, and I felt my emotions well up inside of me. I couldn't take any more, so I walked out. Standing in the street, drawing on a fag, I wondered why I couldn't just be a normal father instead of a drunkard? What was wrong with me?

# 9

# Meeting the Guv'nor

I knew that if Laura divorced me, my life would fall apart, but what I couldn't see then was that it already had fallen apart. I saw her, my four kids and the world through an alcoholic haze. Deep down, I knew that the drink was destroying my life.

Laura tried everything she could to help me. She'd even persuaded me to go and see a counsellor at a private hospital in the West End after hearing a commercial on LBC Radio. But after half an hour of sitting in a consulting room with him, I wanted to knock him spark out. He started bringing up my childhood. What did I feel about my father? What did I feel about my mother? Was I a happy child? When I stood up to go, he asked me for a hundred quid. It was outrageous. I told him to get stuffed and stormed out in a rage. As soon as I got back to Leyton I went straight into the King Harold pub and got drunk.

I'd also been to an Alcoholics Anonymous meeting at Whipps Cross Hospital, although I only went to keep Laura sweet. When I walked into the room and saw all these people sitting there drinking tea, I thought, this isn't for me. Like everyone else there, I stood up and introduced myself. I had a black eye from a fight I'd been in a couple of nights before. 'My name's Alan Mortlock, and I'm an alcoholic,' I said. But I never went back.

I did, however, attend weekly counselling sessions at the mental health unit at Thorpe Coombe Hospital in Walthamstow, and Laura came with me each time. When the counsellor asked me how much I was drinking a week, and I replied about a hundred pints, she nearly fell off her chair. She told me that the pains I was getting in the backs of my calves were common among heavy drinkers and that it could be the onset of something serious.

The counsellor gave me a chart to put on the wall and to make a mark every time I had a drink. I actually stopped drinking completely for three months, and I hated every minute of it. But in the end I felt I couldn't take any more. I felt bored – and went on a massive bender.

Christmas was approaching and we had hardly any money. The drinking had taken away my drive to work when I got up in the mornings, and I was worried about how I'd be able to buy the children their presents. I knew that I needed to stop drinking, but I was unable to. Yet I wanted to. I was in emotional turmoil. My mind was all over the place, and deep down I felt that I was starting to lose the plot big time. I knew that if I saw someone else behaving the way I was, I'd have thought, what a waster.

One Saturday morning, a card dropped through the letterbox. Laura opened, read it, and then walked into the living room, where I was sitting on the floor, wondering whether or not to go to a plastering job I'd landed in Chingford. She threw the card down to me and said, 'Read this.'

It was a religious Christmas card. Written inside were the words, 'Love, peace and joy to you all. Yours in the name of Jesus Christ, Steve, Christine and family'. Steve had also put a small Christian booklet in with the card, but I threw it to one side. Well, maybe he really had got religion, then, I thought. If that's what he wants to do, then good luck to him. It was all nonsense as far as I was concerned.

I decided in the end to go to the job in Chingford and took Adam with me. As I was plastering, though, those words on the card hit me. Peace, love and joy. My family had no love, no peace and no joy. We had turmoil, hatred and misery.

I got back home that evening to find Steve sitting in the kitchen with Laura. I will never forget the day. It was Saturday 15 December 1990.

'Al, what's wrong with you, mate,' he said, smiling and shaking my hand. 'You look rough.'

I shrugged my shoulders and sat down. Laura made us a cup of tea and then left us alone and went into the living room.

Steve knew me well. We'd been through a lot together in the past. One time, we were both pulled in for questioning by the Old Bill after a mate of ours stabbed a bloke to death. I remember another time when he banged at the door one morning at the flat in Seymour Gardens and told me that Customs and Excise were on their way to raid him. He advised me to get rid of any gear I had, to be on the safe side. And when the Old Bill had turned over my flat looking for that gun, they also turned over Steve's flat. They thought they'd found the gun in his flat, but it was actually a cigarette lighter.

Steve began to tell me about how he had been nicked for being caught with forty grand of amphetamine sulphate. When he'd asked for bail, it was refused, as he'd already had several convictions for drug importation and supply, and he was sent on remand to Wormwood Scrubs. He admitted that he was worried that he was going to go down for six years.

Before he was sent down, he continued, a woman who worked at the hospital, where he went for treatment after breaking his arm, had kept on at him to go to church. So one day he went with his wife and children to an Anglican church in Custom House, liked it, and started going each week. But he was still selling drugs.

'Sitting in the cell, Al, I felt my back up against the wall,' he continued. 'So I asked Jesus to come into my life. I only did this because I didn't want to be in prison. Although I'd been going to church, singing the hymns and putting money in the collection plate, I'd never really asked Jesus to come into my life. I then made a promise to God that I wouldn't sell any more drugs.

'I'd had this really bad stomach ulcer for ages. It was agony sometimes, and it had started to get really bad in the Scrubs. About an hour after asking Jesus to come into my life I asked him to take the pain of the ulcer away. When I woke up the next day, the pain had disappeared.'

I wasn't sure what to make of this, so I just nodded.

'There was a Bible in the cell, so I started reading it. I read the whole New Testament over ten days. Now, that's quite a feat for someone like me. When I finished it, I had this strong feeling that I was going to get bail. Then a couple of days later, guess what happened?'

'What?'

'I was given bail. Amazing, isn't it!'

'Straight up?'

He started grinning. 'Yeah. I had twenty-eight grands' worth of gear stashed in a safe at a car workshop on an industrial estate in Barking. When I came out, I sold a couple of grands' worth, but felt bad about this because I'd made a promise to God. When my vicar came to see me, I told him about the drugs and that I didn't know what to do with them. So he knelt down in the living room and started praying about it. And as he did, I felt that I should put the drugs down the toilet. We then drove in his car to the car workshop, collected the gear, went back to his house, and flushed it down the toilet.'

I laughed at this image of the vicar and Steve with the powder. 'It's a good job the Old Bill didn't turn up, isn't it, or the vicar might have been nicked.'

Then, becoming serious, he said, 'Al, you need Jesus.'

'You what?' I laughed, thinking he had gone wonky. He was the last person I thought would become a religious nutter.

He gave me a serious look. 'You need Jesus. He can set you free.'

'Listen, Steve, I don't want to hear this nonsense,' I said, getting agitated.

'Al, believe me. Jesus can set you free,' he repeated urgently. 'Look, I didn't really want to come round, but Laura insisted. She told me you were killing yourself through drink.'

Oddly, Steve hadn't sworn once. I found this strange as he had a real foul mouth, even worse than me. What's more, he didn't have his usual arrogance about him. Instead, there was what I can only describe as a softness about him – a real conviction about what he was saying about this Jesus.

He then rummaged in his shellsuit pocket and pulled out some photocopies of an article called 'Cockney Christians' and handed it to me. 'Read this,' he said.

I glanced at the photocopies and saw the names of Jimmy Tibbs, who was Nigel Benn's boxing trainer, and who in the 1960s had had a reputation on the streets and had done ten years inside following an East End feud, and Benny Stafford, who was one of the well-known Stafford family from Canning Town. His son had fought as an unlicensed boxer for Charlie Smith in the early 1980s.

I sat there and read silently about how their lives had been in turmoil until one day someone told them about Jesus, and how they were now Christians. Benny Stafford had been the first to become a Christian. He'd then told Jimmy Tibbs about Jesus, and eventually he too became a Christian. I saw parallels between their lives and my own life. Interesting, I thought, but not for me.

But I figured that this Christianity lark might provide a way of Laura not divorcing me and give me some time. If I make out I'm going to be a Christian, I thought, she might not ask me to go.

'Okay, Steve, what do you have to do to become a Christian?' I said. 'I'll give it a go.'

'You've got to get down on your knees first and ask Jesus into your life.'

'No way! I ain't getting down on my knees for anyone,' I retorted. 'I've never got on my knees for the Old Bill or anybody. What do you want me to get down on my knees for?'

'Al, Jesus will set you free.' His eyes lit up. 'Imagine a court tearing up your criminal record to give you a new start. If you ask Jesus to come into your life and forgive you, he'll forgive you and give you a new start.'

Although I didn't believe a word of it, I said, 'All right then. I want to go and tell Laura.' I reckoned that all this Jesus stuff was exactly what I needed to buy time with Laura. We then went into the living room, where Laura was sitting on the settee, staring at the TV, and I said, 'I'm going to become a Christian.'

She gave a hollow laugh and her eyes remained glued to the TV. She didn't need to speak – her look said it all.

'But you don't have to do it,' I said.

'Laura, you need the peace of Jesus,' said Steve. 'Let me pray with you.'

'I'm Jewish. I don't believe in Jesus,' she said, looking up at him. Because she'd been to a Roman Catholic convent school, she knew a little bit about Christianity.

Steve shook his head. 'It doesn't matter. Jesus was a Jew.'

Now, to me, prayer was something you did beside your bed when you were a kid, although I'd never done it myself. So I didn't really know what he was on about.

Laura eventually agreed to let Steve pray for her, but I could tell that she was nervous. He closed his eyes, placed his right hand on her shoulder, raised his head upwards and said, 'Lord, I ask you to touch Laura tonight and give her that peace which surpasses all understanding. I ask for the peace of Jesus to come on her now.'

I watched with a mixture of embarrassment and awkwardness, thinking that Steve really had become a Christian. I couldn't believe it.

'Give her peace, Lord. Give her peace,' he kept repeating, his voice rising. And then he started talking in a strange language. This was weird, I thought. What was he talking about?

What happened next was unbelievable. Before my eyes, Laura was transformed from a red-eyed, miserable wreck to a woman who looked so content. Her face was radiant. This is incredible, I thought. She looks like a completely different woman.

'Do you want some more?' asked Steve.

'Yes,' she nodded.

'Lord, fill her up. Fill her up until she overflows,' he continued.

Laura couldn't stop smiling. Eventually she said excitedly, 'It was as if an electric power went right through my body, from my head to my toes. And I could feel all my anguish, pain and sadness going as this power went through.'

'You look completely different,' I said, still trying to work out what on earth was going on.

'I've never felt like this in my entire life. I feel brand new,' she beamed.

I knew that there was something strange going on here, but I couldn't work out what.

'Do you want to give your lives to Jesus?' asked Steve boldly.

We both nodded and then the three of us knelt down on the Chinese rug. I still felt embarrassed, and I didn't really know what I was doing. But something was happening, and I knew from those seances that my mum and dad used to have that there were strange supernatural forces out there.

Steve knelt down with us and then said, 'What I'm going to do now is say the prayer of repentance and I want you to repeat it after me. Through this prayer you'll ask God to forgive you for everything you've ever done wrong. He'll forgive all your sins and then give you a new start and a new life.'

He then produced a Bible from his pocket, opened it, and pointed his finger at a page. 'In the Gospel of John in the Bible, Nicodemus went to Jesus in the middle of the night and said that he knew he was sent by God. Jesus then turned round to him and said that he had to be born again to inherit the kingdom of God.'

'OK,' I said. Laura and I then repeated after him the prayer of repentance: 'Lord Jesus, I come to you tonight as a sinner and I ask you to forgive me for everything I've done wrong. I open up my heart and ask you to come and live inside of me, to guide me, help me, and give me a new life. Thank you, Lord. In the name of Jesus, Amen.'

We then stood up. I really wanted Steve to go now. It was about midnight and I felt I'd had enough of all this Christianity. I was a bit confused by it all. Laura had experienced something, but nothing had happened to me.

'I want to go to bed now, Steve.'

'Al, you need deliverance,' he replied solemnly.

'What's deliverance?' I asked. 'Are you on about that film with Burt Reynolds about the hillbillies?'

'No, Al. You need to have a deliverance prayer because of all the things you've been involved in. I'll talk to you more about that tomorrow.' He then left.

Laura and I sat down in the living room, trying to take it all in. 'So what do you reckon? What was that about?' I said.

'I don't know,' she replied. 'Something strange happened. And I feel so different. But I don't know what it was. Was that really Steve White?'

I nodded. 'I know.'

'He was so different to the way he normally is.'

We then went to bed. In the early hours of the morning I woke up abruptly, and I found myself thinking about what had happened when Steve came round. Then, in the right-hand corner above me, I saw what I can only describe as a sort of haze. It looked similar to cigarette smoke. What's that? I thought. Am I seeing things? And as I looked at it I saw the eyes, nose and mouth of a man looking down at me. He seemed to be smiling. Next to this face was a horrible-looking black bat-like bird. I'm going mad, I thought, sitting up. Laura was fast asleep, and I touched her shoulder to make sure I was awake. The landing light was on and I could hear the kids breathing in the next room and the sound of my dog asleep on the landing. What was happening? Then, slowly, the bat-like bird started to fade away.

I lay there, feeling both excited and scared. I knew that something not of this world was occurring. The next thing I knew, two hands were holding my head, but I couldn't see anyone there. With the hands still on my head, I then felt something I'd never experienced from either drink, drugs or any emotion. I felt a peace, happiness and a joy, and I felt that as this feeling went through my body I was being cleansed. It was like wearing soaking wet overcoats and then having them taken off you one by one. I didn't want it to stop. It was fantastic! I then heard an audible man's voice say to me, 'You're going to be all right, son. You're going to be all right.' It was a reassuring, friendly, authoritative voice. And then I went back to sleep.

In the morning, I came downstairs and went into the kitchen, where Laura was sitting at the table. I felt completely different and, because of that voice I'd heard, I felt that, despite my drinking, drug taking and the rows we'd had, our marriage would be okay. I felt in control. I sat down opposite Laura and told her about the strange events in the middle of the night. She listened, not knowing what to make of it.

I had expected her to be happy, but she didn't seem to be. We then got into an argument about some of the things I had done to her and I found myself shouting at her. I then let out a huge roar, like a lion. Immediately afterwards, I said calmly, 'It's going to be all right, love.' And at that moment I knew inside that things had changed.

Half an hour later there was a knock at the door. I opened it to find Steve standing there. 'I just came round to see how you both are,' he said a little bit sheepishly.

'Come in, mate. Something really strange happened to me in bed last night.'

'I know.'

'You don't sound surprised,' I said.

'I'm not, Al. When I left your place last night I prayed for you as I drove down Grove Green Road. I said, "Lord, Alan needs deliverance, but I'm too scared to give it to him myself." And I felt the Lord say to me that he was going to do it.'

After I'd told him about what had happened in the middle of the night, he said, 'That was the power of Jesus delivering you.'

I just thought to myself, 'What's going on? What's it all about?'

# 10

# On the Firm

'Okay, Al?' asked Steve, nudging me gently.

I shook my head. 'Nah, man, it's not my cup of tea,' I said in a low voice. 'I don't know what they're on about. What's going on?'

I was sitting in a small church in Canning Town. Some of the congregation, which was mainly black, were talking in a strange language, while others were falling on the floor and hollering and shouting. I'd never seen anything like it, and I felt very uncomfortable. I stole a glance at Laura and I could tell she felt the same. When Steve had told us we needed to go to church, I agreed, but if this is what it was going to be like, he could forget it. That church service in Wormwood Scrubs had been bad enough, but this was worse. For a moment, I wondered if the congregation was on speed.

'Let's go then,' said Steve, getting up and motioning to the door. 'I'll take you to another church that might be more up your street.'

'Well, what did you make of that?' I asked Laura as we drove Steve.

'It frightened me, Al,' she replied.

We then drove to a small Baptist church in the back streets of Custom House. The service was very low key and it was a mixed congregation. A fat guy with a dodgy haircut and thick glasses seemed to be running things, and I found myself thinking that he looked a right wimp. I didn't feel that I'd anything in common with the people sitting around me, and when we came out, I told Steve how I felt.

'I don't reckon this one either, Steve. It's not me.'

'OK, Al. Don't worry. There's lots of different types of churches. You've just got to find one that suits you. Come with me to a service on Christmas Eve.'

I still had major money worries, and I'd no idea how I was going to be able to buy presents and all the other things that go with Christmas. I even thought about asking Laura's dad if he'd lend me some money, but I soon dismissed this idea, out of pride.

A few weeks before in the *Walthamstow Guardian*, I'd advertised my services as a builder but, disappointingly, I hadn't had a single phone call. However, the day after I'd been to the church in Custom House a bloke phoned and asked me if I'd take out some fireplaces and do some plastering at his house in Chingford. I leapt at the opportunity. Steve, who also did a bit of building work, along with running his car repair shop in Harold Wood, came on the job with me. I finished it in three days, got paid in cash, and was then able to go and buy presents, a turkey and all the other things we usually had at Christmas.

As I was coming out of the HSS hire shop in High Road, Leytonstone, I heard a car hooting, and then Colin, a black guy I knew from drinking in the King Harold, pulled up in his Golf GTI convertible.

'How's it going, Al?' he grinned, getting out of the car. 'What you been up to?'

We began chatting. As he talked, I noticed that I felt uncomfortable with the fact that when he spoke, every second word was a swear word.

Then I said, 'I've met the guv'nor.'

'What do you mean, you've met the guv'nor? Who?' said Colin.

'I've found Jesus, man. The real guv'nor.'

He looked puzzled.

'No, straight up. I've given my life to Jesus. He's set me free. Something incredible happened to me last night. I'd never have believed it before, but it's true, man, Jesus has set me free.' I could see, though, that he still thought I was off my rocker.

When I started to tell him about the extraordinary events of the night before, his eyes glazed over and he made an excuse that he had to be somewhere. Well, I thought, as I watched him drive off, that's what I would have done last week. I don't blame you, mate.

Late at night on Christmas Eve, Steve took me to a service at the Church of the Ascension, a big, old Anglican church, in Custom House. Laura had to stay at home with the children. After my experiences in Forest Gate and Custom House, I wasn't sure what to expect.

It felt eerie walking through the doors of a church late at night, and the first thing that struck me was the musty smell. The church had a high roof and huge round pillars.

This service was completely different again. It was much more like what I imagined a church service to be. There was a vicar in a dog collar and long, white robes; Bible readings; an altar with candlesticks on it; and an organist. There were probably about 150 people there. As I listened to the vicar give a short sermon, and looked up at the tall grey arches and pillars, I reflected that this time last year I would have been getting out of my brain in a pub. If someone had said to me that I would be in a church the following year, I would have laughed in their face. Afterwards, a number of people came up to me and introduced themselves.

As we left, I said to Steve, 'Aren't these nice people?'

He grinned. 'They are, Al.'

Laura, the kids and I had the best Christmas Day for many years. Unlike other years, Laura and I didn't have any arguments, which were usually caused by me arriving home drunk at 6 a.m. and not being able to eat the Christmas dinner she'd cooked for me, because I was hung over. We had peace in the family, and I didn't have a single drink. I did decide to roll a joint, though, but as I did, I felt it was wrong. I still smoked it, but I never got stoned. I think this was the Lord showing me that I didn't need drugs.

Before I'd seen Christmas as a tradition, but now I was looking at it in a new light. So this image of baby Jesus in the manger wasn't a fairy tale, after all, I found myself thinking. It was actually true that God became a human being. It was mind-blowing stuff. There was an old film about Jesus on TV, and I watched it with fascination.

One afternoon in January, I went with Steve to a car auction in Bow. Even though I was still banned from driving, after the car chase that ended up in Eastern Avenue, I thought it would be interesting. Cars have always been a passion of mine.

'That's a nice motor,' I said, pointing to an automatic burgundy Austin Princess.

'Do you like it?'

'Yeah.'

'I'll buy it for you then.'

'You what?'

'I'll buy it for you. Laura can drive it.'

'No,' I protested.

'Al, you and Laura need a car. Don't worry about it.'

This was so unlike the old Steve. I didn't know what to say. 'Listen, then, I'll pay you back when I get some money.'

'Forget it, Al,' he said, leading me towards the Princess. But I did pay him back, some months later.

I felt that I should look around for other churches in the area, but which one? I liked the Anglican service, but I wanted to find out what else was on offer. So the next day, I went to the Good News shop on High Road, Leyton, to see if they could suggest a church for me to go to. I'd passed this shop countless times in the past, and I remembered when it used to be a tobacconist's.

When I entered the shop I was confronted by Bibles, Christian books, videos, cards, posters, banners with 'Jesus is Lord' written on them, and all sorts of things. It all seemed very strange.

'Are you born again?' asked the owner, a middle-aged woman, coming up to me.

'Yeah, a few days ago I gave my life to him,' I said, and then told her about the night Steve came round.

She smiled and said, 'Praise the Lord.'

I smiled back, thinking that 'Praise the Lord' sounded a very odd thing to say. It reminded me of those nutty preachers you saw in films.

'What church do you go to?'

'I don't have a church at the moment, but I'm looking for one. Do you know of one, then?'

She took a brown paper bag from under the counter and began writing on it. 'Here are a few local ones that you might like.'

I thanked her and went home. I looked at the list of churches and decided that on Sunday I'd check out the Elim Pentecostal Church in Morley Road, Leyton. I didn't know why I chose this one – I just did.

The following Sunday I went there with Steve. The church was a small red-brick building, and as we walked in, a man grabbed hold of me and gave me a hug. What's going on? I thought, trying not to show how embarrassed I felt.

I liked the atmosphere immediately and felt a warmth from the congregation there. Halfway through the service a Canadian man began to preach. He seemed to go on for ages and I didn't have a clue what he was going on about, but judging by the reactions of the people sitting around me, he was having quite an impact. As for me, I was bored and restless.

At the end of the service, a number of people came up to me and shook my hand, and someone invited me to a men's breakfast the following Saturday morning in the church. It sounded interesting, so I agreed to go. If nothing else, I would have a free fry-up, I thought.

Disappointingly, there was no fry-up at the men's breakfast, which was held in the room at the back of the church. Instead, we had cereal, toast and tea. The fifteen or so men there were all very friendly, but I felt out of place, although, at the same time, excited. I listened with interest as they talked about how they saw God at

This is me, aged four, sitting between my
Mum and Dad, with relatives.

Not to be messed with: my skinhead days.

Laura and me on our wedding day, 14 February 1976.

On holiday with (from left) Adam, Sean, Laura and Jamie. This is the
Ford Escort I crashed on the way back from seeing Barry the Hat.

(From left) Adam, Sean and Jamie, just back from karate.

Two family portraits. First, the day Mel was born in 1986;
Laura receives a visit from Sean (pulling a face as usual),
Jamie, Adam and me. The second photo shows us today;
me and Laura with (from left) Mel, Sean and Jamie.
Second photo © Charles Albert.

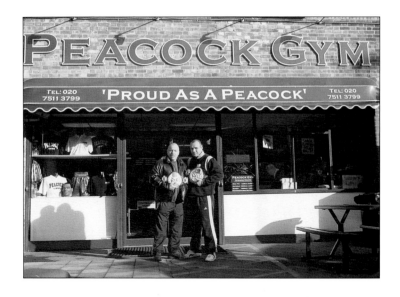

Scenes from the Peacock Gym. Jason Guiver and me, with Jason's
IBA World and British Super Cruiseweight Championship belts.
Below, we are joined in the ring by Mickey Tingey.

I will always pray with my team and our fighter before a fight.
Here, myself, Mickey, Jason and Stacy Dunn ask for the Lord's
protection (top) before Stacy's fight against Colin Blair (below).
Both photos ©Charles Albert.

There is never a wrong time to pray and we do so
here again in a break between rounds (top). Below, referee
Gary Bedford announces Stacy the winner.
Both photos © Charles Albert.

This is a get-together of some of the IBA fighters. There are too many to mention them all, but in the front row (from left) are: Mickey Tingey, Roy 'Pretty Boy' Shaw (with fists clenched), Jason Guiver (pale suit), me, Hughie 'The Banger' Robinson, John Hawkins and Harry the Greek. © Charles Albert.

work in their lives, but, as with the Canadian preacher, I didn't understand the jargon they used, such as 'salvation', 'redeemed', 'on fire', 'discernment' and 'under the blood of Jesus'.

A man called Mervyn Tilley introduced himself to me as the pastor of the church, and I liked him straightaway. He wasn't at all what I'd expected. He was down to earth and seemed a very shrewd and wise bloke.

'You're not wearing a dog collar,' I remarked.

Smiling, he replied, 'I do wear a dog collar — but I keep it for fancy dress parties.'

I also met a man called Bill Gracey, who began to tell me about his faith. A former merchant seaman who'd been brought up a Roman Catholic, he'd had a dream one night and, as a result, became 'born again'. I didn't really understand most of what he was saying, but I listened politely, even though he did go on a bit. I thought he was potty, to be honest.

A few days later Bill turned up at my house one evening. I was a bit surprised to see him, but I invited him in. Laura and I then sat up until about 3 a.m., as Bill patiently explained the key beliefs of Christianity to us. Quoting from the Bible, he told us that God created the earth and everything on it and also created Adam and Eve. He then said that Jesus Christ, God the Father, and the Holy Spirit were not three Gods, but one.

'How do you mean?' I asked. This was hard to get my head round.

'Well, think about water. It can come out of the tap, but when you put it in the fridge, it becomes ice, and if you put it in the kettle, it becomes steam. But it's all the same water,' he said.

He added that Jesus, by dying on the cross to take the punishment for our sins and then being resurrected to show that he had defeated death, acted as a bridge between us — sinners — and God the Father. When Jesus went back to heaven, Bill said, God then sent the Holy Spirit to help us. It was like a complete crash course in Christian theology and I was absolutely fascinated by what I heard, even though I didn't understand a lot of it.

I lay awake in bed that night, thinking that it all sounded too good to be true. I thought about some of the blokes I'd beaten up, my heavy drinking, the way I'd made Laura and the boys suffer, and some of the strokes I'd pulled. I thought of the money I'd wasted on drink and drugs – and the selfishness. Could God really forgive me for all of this? Could I really make a new start in life? I wanted to believe he could.

The next day, I went back to the Good News shop and bought a small pocket Bible, and began to read it as soon as I got home. Mervyn had recommended that I start with the New Testament and then dip into Genesis and some of the other books of the Old Testament.

One of the Bible passages that really hit me was Proverbs 23:29–35 (New Living Translation):

Who has anguish, who has sorrow, who is always fighting, who is always complaining, who has unnecessary bruises, who has blood shot eyes?

It is the one who spends long hours in the taverns, trying out new drinks. Don't let the sparkle and smooth taste of wine deceive you.

For in the end it bites like a poisonous serpent; it stings like a viper. You will see hallucinations, and you will say crazy things. You will stagger like a sailor tossed at sea, clinging to a swaying mast.

And you will say, 'They hit me, but I didn't feel it. I didn't even know it when they beat me up. When will I wake up so I can have another drink?'

When I read this, I was amazed that something written thousands of years ago could be so relevant today. That passage summed up exactly what it's like to be a slave to drink.

I'd always thought of Jesus as someone in a long white robe who wandered around being a boring goody-goody, but when I read the Gospels a very different Jesus emerged. I saw that he was tough, no mug, and, in the way he went to his death on the cross, very courageous. And he held the respect of those around him. I liked the time he turned the tables over in the Temple and told the money-changers to get out. Reading about St Paul, I was impressed by his zeal for telling people about Jesus. There was a lot that I couldn't understand in the Bible, but I didn't care. I just believed. I knew Jesus was real.

I felt I had walked into a new life. Gone were the violence, the raging anger, the pubs, the clubs, the drugs and the swearing. But when I went to church on the following Sunday, I told Mervyn that I was frightened I was going to lose this new life.

'Alan,' he said. 'Forget about your past. Jesus has forgiven you and he wants you to go forward. The only person who will remind you of your past is the devil. And you have to remind him of his future.'

When I told Mervyn what had happened in the middle of the night after Steve White had left me, he explained that the black bat-like bird represented evil, and that when it vanished God had delivered me.

'But some of the things I've done, Mervyn, have been very bad. You don't know all the other things I used to do.'

'Alan, we're all sinners, but all we need to do is to accept the forgiveness of Jesus. You've had what's known as a road to Damascus experience.'

'What do you mean?'

'Read the Acts of the Apostles. You'll read how Saul persecuted the early Church until, one day, God revealed himself to him on the road to Damascus and he changed his name to Paul. And from that point on he became the greatest Christian missionary ever.'

'Okay, mate. I'll read all about him.'

'God has chosen you for some kind of special work, Alan.'

'Some special work? What do you mean?'

'I'm convinced of it. People who have the kind of experience you have had are very rare. God will use your past life in some way to reach people who have lived a similar life to you.'

I found his words very reassuring, but I still wondered what he was on about when he said that God had some special work for me. What kind of work?

I then asked Mervyn to come and bless our house, because so many bad things had happened there over the years. Apart from my boozing and some of the characters I brought home with me, the previous owner and his daughter were killed when the house caught fire. A man I'd met at the church had told me that a way of spiritually cleansing your home was to have it blessed, so a few days later Mervyn came to bless the house. He went into every room, saying a prayer and reading from the Bible.

Not long after, I was baptised at the church. As I went down the steps into the pool of water and Mervyn and another pastor placed my hands across my chest, Mervyn asked me, 'Do you believe in God the Father, God the Son and God the Holy Spirit?'

'Yeah. I do.'

'You are now going to be baptised and you will be a new person.'

They then placed their hands on my shoulders and plunged me into the water. When I came up, all the congregation was singing 'I Am a New Creation' and clapping. I felt great. Laura then stepped into the pool and she also was baptised.

I started going to church every Sunday, sometimes twice, and also attending a prayer meeting on a Wednesday night. At first, I was unable to pray out loud and wave my hands in the air, as most people did. When I first did it, I felt a bit awkward, but that feeling soon passed when I realised that no one was looking at me.

My life was completely unrecognisable from a few weeks before. I was much calmer, and felt content and at peace with myself.

Laura and I were starting to recapture the sparkle we used to have in our marriage. We started going out as a family again, and the children seemed much happier. One morning, Laura told me that she had just read a passage in the Bible that really spoke to her about me. It was Ephesians 2:1–5, where St Paul talks about being dead through sin and then being brought alive through Christ. She was right. It summed me up perfectly.

Word soon went around on the street that I'd become a Christian, but my mates didn't believe it. They all thought I was doing it to get some money out of the church, and on the grapevine I heard that Laura and I were being called 'Jesus and Mary'.

One afternoon, I was sitting in the living room with Laura when what I can only describe as an oppressive feeling suddenly overcame me. For no reason at all, I felt frightened and in a panic.

'What's wrong, Alan?' asked Laura, looking worried.

'Get away!' I shouted at her, pushing her away roughly. 'Leave me alone.'

'I'm going to phone pastor Mervyn,' she said.

'Jesus, help me!' I cried out, getting down on my knees. Immediately I did this, the feelings left me and I felt normal again.

A short while later Mervyn turned up at the door, wondering what the matter was. When I explained what had happened, he nodded knowingly.

'You've been under spiritual attack,' he explained calmly. 'This happens a lot when people come to know Jesus. When you make Jesus your friend, you make an enemy of the devil. He will try and disrupt your new life with God.'

Soon after, I was invited to Georgie Dice's daughter's birthday party at Haydn's Snooker Club in Chingford. It was packed, and Barry the Hat, Weasel and a lot of my mates from Ilford were there, laughing and joking and knocking them back.

'What do you want to drink, Al?' asked Georgie, coming over to me.

'An orange juice,' I replied.

'What! An orange juice? Are you having me on?'

'No. Straight up. An orange juice.'

Standing at the bar and looking around at all the blokes I knew, I felt very uncomfortable; I didn't feel part of them. On the way home in the car I turned to Laura.

'You know what, Laura?'

'What, Al?'

'I'm glad I don't drink any more.'

One day I was in Gants Hill with Laura when I saw this big black bloke coming towards me. He seemed to be staring at me, so I wondered if I'd upset him at some point.

'Hello, Al,' he said, extending his hand.

It was Es Kaitell, who used to run the doors for me at some of my kick boxing shows. I hadn't seen him since the Pickets Lock show in 1989. 'Hello, mate. I've not seen you for ages. What you been up too?'

'Still running the security firm,' he replied. 'What about you?'

'Well, you're not going to believe this, but I've given my life to Jesus. I'm a born-again Christian.'

His eyes widened. 'And you're not going to believe *this*. So am I.'

I was stunned. 'You're joking.'

The three of us then went to a nearby cafe and Es told us that one night he'd gone to Ilford Palais to demand an apology from the doormen who had insulted his friends. They attacked him with baseball bats and left him unconscious and in a pool of blood. His skull was fractured, his jaw knocked out of place, and his left eye damaged. The result of this was that he was unable to eat solids, suffered terrible headaches, and had started to go deaf. One day, he decided to put out a contract on the doormen.

'Then Ian, one of my doormen, invited me to go with him to Kensington Temple in Notting Hill Gate. He'd told me that there was an American preacher coming. Sitting on the tube, Ian told me that I had to forgive the doormen. When he said this, I felt angry. Why was he was taking their side? By the time we reached Kensington Temple, I was raging and in no mood for a church service. Then an amazing thing happened.'

'What?' I asked.

'This feeling of peace came over me and all my anger disappeared. And I forgave the doormen! We then went inside and sat at the back. The place was packed. This American on the stage started preaching, and halfway through he said there was a man in the congregation who'd been badly beaten up six months before. He went on to say that the man had pains in his head, blurred vision, deafness and couldn't eat properly. I knew he was talking about me. He then said, "The Lord thanks you for forgiving," and added that the Lord was going to heal the man. My mind was racing, and I didn't even know if I believed in God. He then asked those with injuries to stand up. Without thinking, I did. I felt this intense heat go through the whole of my body. I thought to myself, what's going on? I felt so much, peace, love and warmth.'

'That's incredible, mate!' I said.

'Yeah, but listen to this, Al. When I went into the lobby area, I suddenly realised that the pains in my head, the blurred vision and my deafness had gone. And I could eat properly too. I went straight back into the hall and raised my hands and shouted, "God, I believe you're real", and I became a Christian from that moment.'

When he'd finished his story, I shook my head in disbelief. 'Well, Es, there's only one thing I can say, man. Praise Jesus.'

I hadn't been into a pub for months, but I decided that I should go to The King Harold to collect an expensive leather punch bag and some pads and gloves I'd left in the room upstairs where I used to train kick boxers. Steve White agreed to come with me. The first thing that hit me when I walked through the doors was the smell of stale alcohol. The regulars greeted me and asked why I hadn't been in for such a long time, so I told them I'd found Jesus. Some of them already knew this, but they didn't know what to say. They probably thought I was mad.

When I came back out I said to Steve, as I put the gear in the boot of the car, 'How did I used to drink in there? How did I stand there for hours on end?'

And I then realised how much time – and money – I'd wasted in pubs. Sometimes I'd look at the clock in a pub and see that it was 11.30 a.m., and then I'd look at it again and see that it was 11.30 p.m. It's funny how time seems to go so quickly when you're drinking in a pub. It felt as if a blindfold had been taken away from my eyes.

When I got home I decided to get rid of my old leather jacket as it reminded me of my old life. I took it out of the cupboard and was immediately hit by the smell of stale alcohol and nicotine. I checked the pockets in case there was a few quid in them, then found a leaflet in the inside pocket. It was a Bible tract. Then I remembered the man who stopped me in Leyton that afternoon a long while back. Amazingly, it had been in my pocket all this time.

I wanted to put something on the front door to let people know we were Christians as I felt that this was important. So I got a friend to paint 'Jesus is Lord' on it. We also started putting church posters in the window.

One evening, there was a knock at the door and I opened it to find a bloke called Tony there. I hadn't seen him for a year or so, but I knew that he was still as violent now as he was back then. Most people were scared stiff of this lump of twenty stone of raging anger. What did he want?

'What's all this about, then?' he asked with a sneer, looking at the poster.

'I've become a Christian, mate.'

He laughed sarcastically. 'Are you having me on?'

'No. It's true. I've got Jesus in my life.'

He looked hard at me and then said, 'My name is Legion and we are many.'

I'd been reading the Bible every day, and I knew that what Tony had said was a quote from Mark's Gospel where Jesus goes to the territory of the Gerasenes and meets a man with an unclean spirit. I thought to myself that this was it; he was going to go for me. I tensed myself, knowing that if we had to fight, he was the type of man who you'd have to seriously damage to stop him killing you. I didn't want to do this, but I'd have to defend myself. But instead he just turned and walked off. Going back inside, I prayed to God not to let Tony come round to the house again. He never did, and when I saw him in the streets he was as good as gold.

Laura and I had started praying regularly together and found it very powerful and a good way of strengthening our family life. After a few months, we decided to hold a prayer meeting in our house. When I asked Mervyn what he thought of the idea, he was very enthusiastic. The meeting went really well, and after Bible readings and a discussion we would sing some songs and then pray. At the end, we all had sandwiches and tea together.

One night, when Laura and I were having a meal in a Chinese restaurant, I felt a desire to tell Terry Buttwell, who'd run the kick boxing gym with me at Cathall Road Leisure Centre, about Jesus. It was strange to find myself suddenly thinking of Terry, as I hadn't seen him in two years due to a falling-out. So when we got home I wrote him a letter and posted it to a sports centre in south-east London, where I knew he was working as a Thai boxing trainer. We met up a few days later and he was intrigued by what had happened to me, and agreed to come to church on Sunday.

When we entered the church, I told Terry to relax as the people here were a great bunch. Terry seemed to enjoy the service, and a few weeks later he too gave his life to Jesus.

One Sunday evening, Terry and I were sitting in the church waiting for the service to start when, out of the blue, a short, fat man with greasy hair and thick glasses, who was sitting in front of me, turned around and said, 'Are you all right, slime hound?'

'What did you say?' I asked, taken aback.

'I said are you all right, slime hound,' he repeated with a sickly grin and then turned around.

'What does slime hound mean?' I said, thinking this didn't sound a Christian term.

'It means toe rag.'

'Toe rag! What, he called me a "toe rag"!' I could feel myself getting up out of the seat to punch the geezer, when Terry put his hand on my arm in a friendly way.

I leaned forward and said to the man, 'God bless you with wisdom, my friend.'

Afterwards, I told pastor Mervyn what the man had said and that I'd wanted to smash him in the face. Mervyn didn't seem surprised, and told me that the man was a bit odd and that he'd speak to him about his behaviour.

I increasingly felt that God was calling me to tell people about him. One night I went into Hobnobs wine bar in Gants Hill to see who was about. At the bar were Harry Curtis, my accountant – a very quietly spoken, smartly dressed man – and Ray Ellis, a builder who was learning to be a surveyor. I'd first met them when I used to drink in The Valentine. After chit-chatting for a while, I told them that I'd found Jesus. As I expected, they were gobsmacked.

Over the following weeks, I made several visits to Harry's office, which was across the road from the wine bar. Ray was often there too, using the computer. Each time, I went there I told them more about Jesus. They were both interested in what I had to say, and a few weeks later agreed to come to church with me, and they also gave their lives to Jesus.

My building work was beginning to really pick up. This was through jobs I got from a number of Elim churches, and as a result of an advert I'd placed in the *Thomson Directory*. I now had a black and silver Ford Transit tipping truck and employed several staff. At times it got so busy that I had to sub-contract work.

I found that now I was a Christian I could do my building jobs much better. Before I would be sloping off to the pub because I didn't want to be on the job. After two or three pints you think you can lay a floor or plaster a wall, but you can't do it properly. But I was never what you'd call a cowboy builder. In other words, I never deliberately ripped people off. Now, though, I'd work through from 7 a.m. to 7 p.m., instead of starting at 10 a.m. and knocking off at 3 p.m.

I remember once when I was building a large extension at a house in Hornchurch, Essex. Ray Ellis, who knew how slapdash I used to be, put the spirit level on the floor and told me I'd done a fantastic job.

'It's not me, Ray. It's the Lord.'

'You reckon,' he said.

'Absolutely, mate. Believe me.'

My faith was really tested in 1991 when my son Adam, then just fifteen, was charged with arson after he set fire to a car after an argument with a geezer in the street. Adam had started getting into trouble a couple of years before when he began playing truant from school and taking cannabis. I'd sometimes leave bits of puff on the mantelpiece and he'd take them.

When I went to see the solicitor he told me that it was a serious offence and Adam could get sent to a young offenders' institution for three or four years. The case rested on the evidence of the witnesses, he explained. From the tone of his voice I knew that what he was really saying was, 'If it could be arranged for the witnesses not to turn up, then he'd get off.'

I knew that I could make sure that the witnesses failed to turn up at court. Nobbling the jury is not uncommon in East London. In other words, the witnesses could be 'visited' by someone and told that it wasn't in their interests to go to court. Or they might be offered what's known as a 'drink' – in other words, money.

The Old Bill phoned me up one day and a voice said, after introducing himself, 'We're warning you not to talk to any of the witnesses in your son's case.'

'You what?' I asked, taken aback. They obviously thought I was still at it.

'If they're interfered with, we'll be round,' said the voice sternly.

I was torn between helping Adam by taking the worldly approach or taking the Lord's way. And although he didn't actually say it, I could tell Adam wanted me to arrange for the witnesses to be nobbled.

'I can stop this now, you know,' I said to Laura.

'So all of this has been a waste of time. None of this is real, then?' she replied.

'What do you mean?'

'What happened to you that night when Steve came round.'

'Course it is.'

'So how can you go backwards, then?'

I didn't know what to say.

'You've got to leave it with Jesus, Al.'

'Yeah, you're right.'

I was at that time building an extension at Wadham Hall Christian Centre in Walthamstow. Working with me were Bill Gracey and a guy called Fergie, who was an ex-heroin addict who'd been healed by the power of Jesus. He was now a member of the Victory Outreach Church in King's Cross.

Bill could see that I wasn't myself. 'What's up, Al?'

I then told him about Adam. 'I can't let my son go to prison,' I said.

'Well, let's pray,' he said, putting down his trowel.

'Yeah, okay.'

The three of us then knelt down and I began to pray out loud. 'Lord, in the old days I'd sort this out myself. But even the solicitor is hinting that Adam will go to prison. Please will you be the judge. You know him. I'm not going to get involved.'

When I got home, I phoned up Mervyn and asked him to ask church members to pray for Adam at the time of his court appearance.

The morning of Adam's appearance at Waltham Forest Magistrates Court for the committal proceedings arrived. As we were leaving the house, he looked at me as if to say, 'Dad, do something.'

I turned to him and said, 'The Lord's going to sort this out.' When we walked into the court I prayed silently. 'Lord, don't let the witnesses turn up. You sort it out.'

Just before 1.30 p.m. we were called into the court. Adam made his way to the witness box, looking nervous, as the charges were read out, then the prosecution barrister stood up and addressed the magistrate.

'Your honour, could we have a bit more time?' he asked.

'Why?'

'Because our witnesses haven't arrived yet.'

'Very well. I'll adjourn the case until 2 p.m.' When he said this, I knew that the Lord was at work.

Just before 2 p.m. we all returned to the court.

'Have you got your witnesses here?' asked the magistrate, addressing the prosecution barrister.

'No. They've not arrived.'

'Well, this isn't very good. They should be here. If they're not here in ten minutes I'm going to dismiss this case.'

The witnesses failed to turn up and the judge threw out the case. As the three of us left the court, I said to Adam, 'You know who did this, don't you?'

'Yeah, dad, I do know. It was the Lord,' he said, looking upwards. No one had nobbled the witnesses, I knew that for sure.

One night, I went to Leyton Town Hall to hear an evangelist called George Miller. The hall was packed. During the service he came up to me and asked me if I wanted to talk in tongues. I'd seen people speaking in tongues at church, but I didn't really understand it. George Miller said that he felt that the Lord wanted to bless me. I stepped forward and stood in a line with a dozen or so other people; George then placed his hands on my shoulders and began praying over me. I found myself praying in a language that I didn't recognise. It was a strange feeling.

Afterwards, someone asked me to stand behind the elderly woman who was standing next to me, as George was going to pray over her. But I was deep in prayer and before I realised what he wanted me to do the woman fell over and landed on her back. Fortunately, she wasn't hurt. In fact, she seemed completely at peace.

One day I was invited to give my testimony at St Mary's church in Walthamstow, so I drove there with Steve White. As we approached the church, I said to him, 'You know what?'

'What, Al?'

'I walked through the graveyard of this church with John Hawkins after we'd been on a session, and I cried out to God, even though I didn't believe in him then. I now know that he heard me, and know he's brought me back to speak for him.'

During my testimony, I felt the Holy Spirit say to me that there was a woman in the congregation who was holding back from giving her life to Jesus. So I stopped speaking and said, 'God's telling me that there's a woman here tonight who wants to give her life to the Lord. He's saying just do it.'

I then heard someone sobbing. Looking around, I realised that it was a woman in her twenties sitting towards the back. I then carried on with my testimony. Afterwards, I stood at the back of the hall and mingled with the congregation.

'Remember me?' asked a middle-aged woman coming up to me.

I looked round. I didn't recognise the woman at all. Standing next to her was the woman who had been crying during my testimony.

'No,' I said, shaking my head.

She grinned. 'You tried to sell me a Volkswagen Beetle once – and I asked for my deposit back because it was no good.'

'Yeah, that's right.' I was gobsmacked and a little embarrassed. In fact, I hadn't been going to give her the money back, but I relented in the end.

She went on to say that she was a member of St Mary's church, but she hadn't really given her life to Jesus, while her daughter rarely went to church. She then asked me if I'd pray with both of them. We went to a room upstairs, where I prayed with them, and they both invited Jesus into their lives.

It was around this time that a screw who also ran a youth club at a church in Mile End invited me to speak to some of the inmates at Pentonville Prison. I spoke to about fifty prisoners in the chapel. After I'd given my testimony I did an altar call and asked those who wanted to accept Jesus into their lives to put their hands up. Quite a few of them did.

The screw then asked me to give another talk at Pentonville, and also do some one-to-one counselling with prisoners who were under rule 43. In other words, they were segregated prisoners. Prisoners are segregated for their own safety – many, but not all, have been convicted of rape or sexual offences against children.

'I can't do it,' I said. I didn't want to meet rapists and nonces.

'Why?' he asked. 'You won't know what they've done unless they decide to tell you.'

'Well, I've got to think and pray about this,' I replied.

I went to see Mervyn and explained my misgivings about the talk.

'Would Jesus go in and speak to them?' he asked.

'Yeah, I suppose so.' I hadn't looked at it like this.

'Very well. Then you go.'

'But I'm not Jesus.'

'Go with the power of God, Al. You're here to do God's work.'

A week or so later I went back to Pentonville. I knew that Mervyn was right, and that Jesus wouldn't reject these men, but I felt uncomfortable.

In a room at the back of the chapel I prayed individually with about ten men. Before I started, I made it clear that I didn't want to know what they'd done. I explained that I was just there to tell them about Jesus and pray with them. I told them I knew how difficult it was to be banged up in prison, and mentioned my spells in Wormwood Scrubs and Camp Hill.

One man, who was about halfway through his sentence, told me that he couldn't take any more of life in prison because he was missing his wife and kids so much. I told him that when he got back to his cell that he should get down on his knees and ask Jesus for help.

A few weeks later a letter arrived for me at the Elim Pentecostal Church in Leyton. It was from this guy. In it, he thanked me for praying with him and said that he'd prayed as I'd told him to. An hour later, a screw opened his cell door and told him he was going home, as his parole had been granted. He explained that he'd been put in segregation because he owed tobacco to some geezers in prison and they were out to get him as he hadn't paid it back. Reading the letter, I felt elated, and thought to myself that I was glad that I'd returned to Pentonville.

My whole attitude to life was completely different to before I found Jesus. For example, one afternoon I took my son, Mel, shopping in Stratford. When we came out of W. H. Smith I noticed that he had a rubber in his hand.

'Did you pay for it, son?' I asked.

He shook his head. 'No, Dad.'

So I went back into the shop and queued up at one of the tills and then gave the sales assistant 13p. In the old days, I'd have seen getting away without paying for it as a result!

Since becoming a Christian I'd wondered what I might do if I found myself in a potentially violent situation, and I prayed regularly that God might give me the grace to control myself. The test came one summer evening when I was returning home. I was halfway down the road where I live when I saw two guys, one black and one white, leaning into the side window of my Ford Escort.

'Oi! What do you think you're doing?' I screamed at the top of my voice.

They looked up and then began sauntering towards me. I could see that they were up for it, but I felt I could easily handle them both. My adrenaline was racing. But as they got a few yards from me I found myself saying, 'You all right, lads?' They looked at me and then at each other, not knowing what to think, and then they walked off.

As I walked into the house, though, I suddenly felt that I wished I'd battered them. I told Laura what had happened. 'I've lost my bottle,' I said.

'No you've not, Al. You didn't thump them because you've found God.'

# 11

# The Publican

I was keen to get back into training kick boxers as I'd really started to miss the fulfilment and buzz it gave me. It was a great feeling to see someone progress from nothing to a competent kick boxer. So I mentioned this one day in late 1993 to Harry Curtis, my accountant.

'Well, Al, you're welcome to use my snooker club to set up a gym. You can have that big room at the back,' he offered.

'Are you sure?'

I knew that Harry's snooker club, Haydn's, in Chingford, was losing a lot of money and that he was losing interest in it. He let the staff run it, and he reckoned that some of them were nicking money. What's more, the regulars were getting free drinks and being allowed to stay after hours.

So I set up a kick boxing gym there, and within a short space of time I had a dozen guys coming along each week. I saw a lot of potential in Haydn's. Situated above a large printer's in Chingford Road, and sandwiched between a car spray shop and a secondhand industrial kitchen equipment outlet, it had two bars, fifteen snooker tables, and two function rooms. It should have been a gold mine.

A few weeks later Harry popped into the gym one afternoon. 'Al, I'm thinking of closing down the club.'

'Closing it? It's a real money spinner, Harry.'

'It's got too many problems. I just want to be rid of it.'

'Why don't you let me run it,' I said.

'Are you serious?'

'I am. I reckon I could turn it around. I'll be your partner, but all you will have to do is the books.' Although I'd never run a club of any description, I felt, with my experience in staging successful kick boxing shows, that I could put Haydn's on the right track. And I'd always fancied running a snooker club.

'Okay, Al. Let's give it a go.'

'Fantastic, Harry.' I was thrilled.

One afternoon a few days later, I accompanied Harry to the club. When we walked in, Paul, the manager, was playing the fruit machine. From his expression, he was clearly taken aback at our unexpected arrival.

'Can you come into the office, mate. I want to have a chat with you,' I said, beckoning him over. Looking worried, he followed us into the small office near the entrance to the building.

'There's going to be some changes,' began Harry.

'Changes?' said Paul meekly, realising that he'd been tumbled.

'That's right. As from now, Alan will be managing the club. I know what's been going on here, Paul. I'm not a mug. You've had your hand in the till, people have been getting free drinks, and you've been serving late.'

Paul looked very sheepish at this and stared at the floor.

'Open the safe, Paul,' said Harry. He did as he was told. Inside were half a dozen bottles of vodka.

'What are these doing here?' asked Harry, annoyed.

'Look, mate, it's on top now. You'd better tell him what you've been up to,' I said.

With tears in his eyes, which I reckoned were moody, he said, 'Okay, I've taken money from the till and I've nicked some bottles of spirits. I'm sorry. I don't know why I did it.'

It turned out that he'd been using bottles of spirits he'd bought at the off-licence, rather than those ordered for the club.

There's about thirty-three measures in a 75 cl bottle of spirits, so by using his own bottles, he was pocketing about fifty quid for himself.

'Right. Well, I'm going to call the Old Bill,' said Harry sharply.

'No, Harry, let's sort this out ourselves,' I said. This sounded too much like grassing to me. 'Listen, Paul, you're finished here after this. Give me the safe keys, get your stuff and go.' In the old days I'd have given him a dig.

He mumbled a thank you and got up and left.

I told Harry that Laura would come in and run the bar. Having worked as a barmaid before, she knew a little bit of what was involved. I then walked around the club to see what improvements needed to be made. It was very tatty and needed a good lick of paint. It occurred to me that, as many of the regulars were football fans, it would be a good idea to install Sky TV. There was a small TV above the bar, but this only showed the terrestrial channels.

So I went up to a group of regulars standing at the end of the bar and asked them if they'd like Sky TV. Not surprisingly, they all thought it was a great idea. So the next day, I went out and bought a large TV for one hundred and fifty quid, and by the end of the week Sky TV had been installed, and I was flavour of the month.

Although I'd spent much of my life propping up bars, I knew nothing about the mechanics of being a publican, so I went to a mate of mine who ran The Higham Hill Tavern in Walthamstow and asked him if he'd come round to explain to Laura what was involved. He agreed, and the next day he took her through changing barrels and optics, cleaning the pipes, ordering the right amount of stock, and so on. She picked it up very quickly.

Initially, I decided to keep the existing half a dozen staff, as I knew that to get rid of them would result in me losing a lot of the regulars – something I couldn't afford to do.

The club opened at 10 a.m. when old-age pensioners used to come in to play snooker at a reduced rate until 2 p.m.

I removed five snooker tables, as they were hardly ever used, and erected a boxing ring instead. To smarten up the club, I took out a wall and replaced it with a glass partition, so people at the bar could see into the snooker room. I also turned one bar into an American theme bar – I bought posters of James Cagney, James Dean, Marilyn Monroe and old Harley Davidsons, along with 1950s signs, such as ones for Coca-Cola, from a memorabilia shop in Wandsworth. Fergie, the ex-heroin addict, painted a New York skyline across one wall and the stars and stripes on the other. I also installed a pool table, juke box, pinball machine, and secondhand Chesterfield settees bought from the Green Man pub in Leyton.

One lunchtime, as I was leaving the club, I met a guy on the stairs. 'Who's the guv'nor?' he asked.

'That's me,' I replied, thinking he looked familiar. 'Don't I know you?'

He smiled. 'I'm Jim McDonald. I want to start a box aerobics class and I wondered if you had any space I could rent.'

Of course! It was Jim McDonald. He'd been the European lightweight boxing champion and had fought two world title fights, one of them against South African Azoomah Nelson.

'Yeah, it would be great to have you run a class here,' I said, thinking that having Jim McDonald involved with the club would be a real feather in my cap.

I then discovered that the drinks licence had run out, so Laura and I applied to Waltham Forest Magistrates Court for a new one. However, before this I had to be interviewed by the Old Bill. Standing outside Chingford nick, I paused and prayed that the Lord's will would be done.

We were shown into a small office, where the licensing officer was sitting behind a desk and another Old Bill was sitting next to him. He looked up from a file he was reading and told us to take a seat.

'You've done about everything here except murder and rape,' he said disapprovingly, pushing the file across the desk towards me.

I looked at the file and saw that it contained a photo of me, details of various convictions I'd received, and information about my spell in prison. I hadn't been expecting this. Even though I'd broken the law quite a few times, I'd never thought of myself as a villain.

'All of this was when I was younger. Isn't everyone entitled to a second chance?' I asked.

'With a record like yours, I'm not sure.'

'Look, I'm a different man now. I'm nearly forty and I put all that stuff behind me when I found Jesus.'

The licensing officer's ears pricked up at this. 'You're a Christian?'

'I am,' I replied, and I then gave him my testimony.

'That's an amazing story. I'm a Quaker.'

'Praise the Lord,' I replied, glancing at the other Old Bill, who remained expressionless.

The licensing officer then looked hard at me and said, 'This club's a bad club. There's drug dealing going on there, stolen goods, fighting. And after-hours drinking.' He paused. 'But you might be just the man to sort it out, so I'm going to recommend to the court that they give you a licence.'

'You are? Thanks.'

'But if you mess me about I'll take it away as quick as I've given it to you.'

'Don't worry, I won't. That kind of life is in my past. I'm walking with the Lord now.'

The licensing officer was as good as his word, and later in the week Laura and I were granted the drinks licence at Waltham Forest Magistrates Court.

My idea was to turn Haydn's from a snooker club into more of a leisure club for families. In order to let people know that new management were now in charge, I held a family open day. I hired a large bouncy castle and put it up next to the car park, while there were demonstrations of boxing and kick boxing in the gym, along with a demonstration from Jim McDonald.

One of the first things I did was put an end to the late-night drinking. In the past, the club had sometimes stayed open until 2 a.m. or even longer. If we were busted for late-night drinking, I knew that that would be the end of my licence.

One afternoon, I walked into a carpet shop near the club, hoping that I could persuade the owner to sponsor a kick boxing event in the gym. I introduced myself and he told me his name was Steve Johnson, who, I later nicknamed Steve the Carpet. He was six foot six, well built, and looked as if he could handle himself.

'If you give me thirty quid, I'll give you an advert in the programme, and I'll throw in some ringside seats at the show free of charge,' I said.

He thought for a moment and then said, 'OK. It's a deal. I'm into boxing.'

We then chatted for a while about the people we both knew. From what he said, he seemed to spend most of his life in the pub, just like I'd done before I became a Christian. I invited him to come to the club for a drink, and left the shop. But then, feeling that the Holy Spirit wanted me to speak to him, I turned around and went back in.

'Can I have five minutes of your time, mate?'

'Of course, man. What is it?'

'I was a bit like you once,' I began. 'I was a big drinker and I did a lot of gear. But something drastic changed my life.'

'Go on, mate, tell me what changed your life, then.'

'Jesus Christ,' I replied, wondering what his reaction would be.

'Really.' I could see that he thought I was a nutter. I then pulled up a chair and told him how Jesus had transformed my life. He listened politely, but I could see he was unimpressed.

Two weeks later, Steve and some mates came to the kick boxing show, and thoroughly enjoyed it. He then started drinking regularly at the club, and I began popping into his shop from time to time. I discovered that when he was younger he'd been a West Ham United football hooligan and had got into a lot of tear-ups with rival supporters. He'd done a bit of door work and had also been a minder and driver for a well-known East End face. He'd ask me questions about my faith and the Bible, but he showed no interest in exploring Christianity for himself.

'It's interesting, Al, but I can't believe in a God who allows so much suffering and evil in the world. And I just see the Church as corrupt. Look at those vicars who get done for abusing kids.'

'Yeah, I know, but this is nothing to do with Jesus. It's man who commits evil, not God. God gives man free will. There's also the devil.'

The first bit of trouble I had to deal with came at a wedding reception one Saturday night. It was a real Essex affair, with about 300 guests, most of them quite loud and flash characters.

'Double whiskey, mate,' said a tall guy at the bar.

As I poured his drink, he began snorting cocaine off the back of his hand.

'What do you think you're doing?' I said angrily.

'What's the matter?' he replied, continuing to snort the cocaine.

My blood was boiling and a part of me wanted to grab him around the neck and haul him over the bar. But instead I prayed for self-control. 'You're taking a right liberty, mate. If you do that again, you're out.'

He shrugged his shoulders, slapped his money down on the counter, picked up his drink, and sauntered back to his table. Looking around the bar, I then noticed four guys at a table in the corner who were also snorting cocaine. I'd have to put a stop to this, but I knew I had to be careful, as I had no doormen to back me up should any trouble start.

I came out from behind the bar and went to the room where the snooker tables were and prayed. 'Lord,' I said, 'I hope I don't have to bash these boys. If I do, I hope you'll forgive me. But I'm not having them taking liberties with me. I won't have any drugs here. I ask you to protect me, Lord.'

I then returned to the bar and made my way through the crowd to where the four guys were sitting. They were about to snort some gear.

'You're taking a liberty. Get that stuff off the table,' I ordered.

'You want a bit, mate?' said one of them, pointing at the table.

'I'm telling you. Get it off the table now. Or you're out,' I repeated firmly.

The four of them could see from my face that I meant business. Obediently, one of them reluctantly brushed the powder off the table.

I then went to have a word with the groom. I told him that we'd worked hard to make his wedding reception a good one and that I wouldn't stand for any of his guests doing drugs in the club. He apologised, and told me that he would make sure it didn't happen again.

It was clear that we were going to have to sort out a few troublemakers in the club. There was a group of blokes who came regularly and had what I would call a footballer/dart player mentality. I mean by this that they were very loud, foul-mouthed and aggressive, and they were into all the communal sing-songs. They thought they could run the place and I knew that it wouldn't be long before there was some major trouble.

The trouble I had been expecting kicked off at a disco one Friday night. My sons, Adam, Sean and Jamie, and his friend, Andrew, were there, along with Steve the Carpet. At one point during the evening an argument broke out between the DJ, who was in his thirties, and Andrew, who was sixteen. Seeing the DJ push him, I came out from behind the bar.

'Oi! Leave him alone. He's only a kid,' I said.

'What's it got to do with you,' sneered the DJ.

'I'm the guv'nor here. That's what it's got to do with me.'

As I said this, one of the regulars, Tim, a black cab driver, grabbed my hand in a friendly manner and said, 'Al, leave it out.'

'Get your hands off,' I snapped, quickly turning round.

He let go and then Jamie and the DJ began pushing and shoving each other. I managed to get them out of the club and down the stairs into the car park.

About fifteen regulars followed us outside. Some of them decided to have a go at Adam, Sean and Jamie, thinking they were only kids. But what they didn't know was that my sons had all done martial arts since they were about six. I watched as they swiftly and expertly went through their moves, knocking down the regulars like skittles. If necessary, I'd join in, but they didn't need me. Then one of the regulars tried to grab Laura, but Steve the Carpet head-butted him and he collapsed on the floor. It was all over in minutes and the regulars slunk off home, humiliated. They were grown men, all in their thirties, and they had been given a hiding by four boys.

When I went back into the club, one of the barmaids asked me what I was going to do about them.

'I'm going to bar them, of course,' I said tersely.

'Well, can I talk to them first?'

'If you want,' I said nonchalantly.

The next day, I was contacted by a number of the regulars who were worried that they might be barred. The club was their life – just as pubs had been my life. I invited them to come and see me, and about a dozen of them did, individually, and each one apologised. I told them they could carry on coming to the club, but if there was any more trouble they'd be barred.

A few nights later, however, I found myself having to deal with a particularly nasty character. Laura was serving behind the bar in the function room, where there was a big darts tournament, and I was serving behind the main bar. There was a store room, where we kept the beer, between the two bars.

Then Laura came bursting through. 'Quick! Al, some bloke's come behind the bar. He tried to grab hold of me. I told him off for swearing at me and he didn't like it.'

Fuming, I stormed into the other bar and found this big geezer behind the bar with another couple of blokes. Seeing that he was hell-bent on a row, I picked up a wine glass and moved towards him. He held his fists up and taunted me.

'Come on then!' I challenged. Just then, I felt the Holy Spirit saying to me, 'Put the glass down.' I did this and stared hard at the man. I could see he wasn't sure what was going on. The two other blokes then grabbed hold of him and took him out from behind the bar.

By now, all eyes were on me. There must have been about eighty blokes there. I reached for the switch above and turned the music off and shouted, 'All you lot aren't worth a tanner. All you're good for is having a go at women. Now get out of my club!'

But they just stood there, smirking. Right, I thought, you're leaving *now*, and I went into the store room to get a big hammer I used to open the barrels.

Tim, the black cab driver, came up to me and whispered in my ear. 'Al, you're a publican now. Put it away. Just call the Old Bill.'

'I've never called the Old Bill in my life,' I replied, knowing that he was right. I left the hammer in the store room and returned to the bar. 'So are you lot going to go or not?'

'We're staying,' bellowed one of them. 'This is our club.'

So I went into my office, closed the door, and phoned the Old Bill. For someone who was used to being on the other side of the law, this was an odd experience.

Half a dozen Old Bill soon arrived and cleared the club. But one bloke called Terry came up to me before he left and said in a threatening voice, 'We're going to do you.'

'You reckon,' I replied, knowing that he was one of those who was all talk. 'We'll see about that.'

I got hold of his phone number and address from a friend and phoned him early the following morning. I knew he would have a big hangover. 'Hello, Terry,' I said brightly. 'How are you?'

'Who is it?' he asked sleepily.

'It's Alan at Haydn's.'

'Alan?'

'Yeah. Now listen, you can meet me with your mates on the green behind the club and I'll take you on one at a time.'

'Alan, I'm sorry. I didn't mean it.'

'You didn't mean it? I'll tell you what, I don't want to see you or your mates at my club again. Got it?'

'Yeah,' he said meekly.

One day, Laura, Sean and I went with Dave Lipscombe and his wife to Jefferson's Bar and Grill in Buckhurst Hill for a meal. I used to buy cars from Dave, who ran a car showroom opposite the club. I'd do them up and sell them on, and sometimes I'd go with him to car auctions. I used to call Dave the old grey fox, because of his silvery hair. We became good mates and we used to spar together in the gym on Saturday mornings.

I'd been looking forward to the meal, as Laura and I hadn't had a day off for weeks. The club was so busy and demanding.

Dave was showing a lot of interest in knowing more about Jesus, and the meal was an opportunity for me to try and answer some of his questions. Just as we were tucking in to our roast beef, my name was called over the tannoy and I was asked to go to the bar.

Wondering what had happened, I went up to the bar. One of the barmaids told me there was a call for me and handed me the phone.

It was Adam, who I had left in charge at the club. He was in a total panic. 'Dad! Dad! Quick. We've got a load of travellers here and they've been rowing among themselves,' he said.

Oh, no, I thought. The first Sunday I've had off in ages and trouble breaks out. 'Tell me exactly what's going on, son.'

'There's about twelve of them and they've smashed the main door.'

'Who's their guv'nor? Describe him.'

'He's stocky, got black hair, and he's wearing a bright mauve shirt.'

'Right, I'm on my way, son. See you in ten minutes.'

I went back to the table. 'I've got to go. We've got trouble at the club. Travellers.'

'Do you want a hand?' asked Dave, getting up.

'It's up to you.'

'Well, I'm coming.'

'And me, Dad,' said Sean.

My adrenaline was pumping during the three-mile journey. As we hurried up the stairs I could hear shouting from the bar. We walked in, I nodded to Adam, and then went straight to the store room and picked up the hammer. I came out and walked towards the travellers. They looked startled. I then walked past them and went downstairs to hammer the panel in the front door back in.

When I walked back into the bar, I could see that the travellers were worried because I was holding a hammer. 'Right, you don't come into my club and start grief.'

'It's all right, mate,' said the traveller in the mauve shirt.

'It's all right? What do you mean "it's all right"? You're causing trouble in my club,' I said, standing in front of them. I could see that they were looking worried. 'Now listen to me. I don't mind you coming to my club to drink – that's what it's here for. But if you cause trouble, you get trouble. Got it?'

He nodded. 'I'm sorry.'

'OK. I'm glad we understand each other.'

Around this time, Sean got expelled from school. The head said he was awkward and that she thought he'd be better suited to another school. Laura and I felt that this wasn't justified and we went to see his head teacher. We learnt that a number of other pupils had also been expelled, but she refused to reverse her decision. In the end, we placed him in another school in Chingford. One lunchtime, he turned up at the snooker club with a worried look on his face.

'What's up, son?'

'A bully picked on me in the classroom.'

'What did you do?'

'I hit him. He said to me that two of his mates are going to stab me at going home time.'

'You what! Who are they?'

'Don't know. But they're older and he reckons they've stabbed people before.'

'Okay, you go back to school and leave it to me. I'll sort it out. I'll be waiting for you outside school.'

Just before home time, I drove there and parked my van up opposite the school gates. I then spotted two big youths sauntering down the road. They were probably about eighteen; they stood smoking by the gates, but they hadn't clocked me, as the road was full of parents' cars. I then heard the school bell go and the first kids started to come out. Soon Sean appeared, and I was just about to get out of the car when I saw Jamie marching down the road with his mate, Andrew, who'd been involved with the fight with the DJ and his mates. Sean must have told him about the threat.

I quickly got out of the van and headed across the road. One of the youths whipped out a long knife and then Jamie pulled out an aluminium baseball bat.

'That's enough!' I yelled, standing between them, then turning to Jamie, Sean and Andrew, I said, 'Get in the van.' The youths looked at me and then walked off. Some years later, I heard that these youths were sent to prison for stabbing someone.

I have never wanted my sons to follow the path I took in my early years, when I was always getting into tear-ups, but I have always wanted them to learn to stand up for themselves and not allow anyone to bully them. Equally, I have taught them never to be bullies.

But there were also some amusing incidents at Haydn's, such as the time when the Christian Businessmen's Fellowship booked the function room for a dinner. Laura and I wanted to impress them and show that Christians could run a snooker club. As usual with events such as this, we hired an outside catering company to provide the food.

It was all going well, and the sixty or so Christian businessmen seemed to be thoroughly enjoying the meal. After they'd finished, they sat there in silence waiting for the guest speaker to take to the floor.

Suddenly, a piercing scream could be heard and one of the waitresses came running out of the kitchen. 'He effing well hit me! He effing hit me!' she screamed.

The businessmen looked aghast. Thinking quickly, Laura put some music on, while I took the waitress back into the kitchen to find out what had happened. It turned out that she'd had an argument with the bloke in charge of the catering and he'd whacked her.

Another amusing incident was when one day I received a phone call from a very posh-sounding bloke. 'I believe you have a boxing ring at the club,' he said.

'That's right,' I replied, thinking he didn't sound like someone who would be interested in boxing.

'Well, another man and I need to settle a grudge in the ring. Would you act as referee for us?'

'Is this a wind-up?' I asked.

'No. We want to settle an argument.'

It was an unusual request, but I agreed to let them use the ring. The next day, two smartly dressed men in expensive-looking suits walked into the club. After they had changed into T-shirts and tracksuit bottoms, I gave them both a pair of gloves and they squared up to each other in the ring. They really went for it, and I found it very funny. Eventually, though, for their own safety, I had to stop the fight, as they were knocking the granny out of each other. They left, appearing satisfied that they had settled whatever grudge they had.

By now, Jim McDonald was training professional boxers in the gym. He had some big names – Scott Welsh, Danny Williams, Julius Francis – and Sky TV crews often came in to do interviews. One day we even closed the gym so that Steve Collins, world super middleweight champion, could train there.

At my next kick boxing show, beside the swimming pool at Epping Forest Country Club, I put some unlicensed boxers on the bill. Keith Butler fought Brian 'The Bull' McHugh, and Kevin 'Geezer' McArthur fought Craig 'The Essex Terminator' Leighton. Seeing how much the audience enjoyed these fights, I decided to include more unlicensed boxers on the bill for the next show.

You come across some interesting characters when you run a snooker club. One evening, I was chatting with a customer when Gary, one of my bar staff, signalled to me from the other end of the packed bar that there was a phone call for me.

'Who is it?' I shouted back above the music.

'He says it's Reggie,' he replied excitedly.

'Reggie? Reggie who?'

He put the phone to his mouth again. And then his mouth dropped open and he was momentarily speechless. 'It's Reggie Kray,' he said eventually. Gary idolised the Krays.

Surprised, I took the phone from a wide-eyed Gary. Reggie was in prison. What did he want? My only link with him had been that time a few years before when I'd been involved in the charity boxing show at Poplar Civic Centre, and we'd sold some of his paintings afterwards at the Lord Raglan.

'Hello, Alan. It's Reggie Kray. How are you, mate? Just ringing to see how Scott's doing for the fight.' Scott Welsh was a young heavyweight fighter who used my gym, and was preparing to fight Joe Bugner. A few years later, he appeared in the film *Snatch* and played the part of a guy who fought the character played by Brad Pitt.

'Okay, Reg.'

'Is he training with you?'

'No, Reg. With Jimmy Mack. But he's always in and out of my gym.'

'Is he there at the moment? I want to wish him good luck for his big fight.'

'No, he's not here, but I'll tell him you called.' After chatting about boxing and my gym, he said goodbye. Some of the regulars standing around the bar had tried to eavesdrop on the conversation, and I could tell from their faces that they expected me to tell them why Reggie had phoned. But I left them wondering.

I was in the gym one afternoon when I noticed something sticking out of a guy's training bag. Surely, it couldn't be, I thought, as I went over to take a closer look. But it was. He had a .38 in his bag. When I asked him what he was doing with the gun, he told me that he'd been threatened and he was carrying the gun for self-protection. Hearing his explanation, I reminded myself that although I had turned my back on violence, I was still moving in a very dangerous world.

# 12

# The Word on the Street

I believe that a Christian, like a boxer, has to train. You can't get into the ring if you're not fit; and likewise, if you don't want to become worldly, you have to keep spiritually fit by praying, reading the Bible, and having fellowship with other Christians. If you don't do this, you find little cracks appearing in your life. In other words, as it says in the Bible, your old self comes back. I believe that for the first year or so of your Christian life the Holy Spirit holds your hand. A pastor I know once put it like this. When you have a child, you hold his hand until he has learned to walk and is aware of the dangers on the roads. This is what the Holy Spirit does to the new Christian, but there comes a time when the Holy Spirit lets go of your hand and you have to walk alone. But he's still there, watching over you.

Being a Christian is not one big spiritual high. You still live in the world and you're still faced with temptations and your weaknesses. Becoming a Christian isn't a cop-out, for in many ways life is harder because you're faced with moral dilemmas that before you wouldn't have given much, if any, thought to. I'm far from perfect, but if I fail I ask Jesus to forgive me, and I try harder next time. But I'm living a more honest and decent life than I did before I became a Christian.

I've never been one for street evangelism as I don't think it's that effective. Often you are drowned out by the sound of the traffic and most people just hurry on past you. It never got me interested in Christianity back in the old days. I prefer a one-to-one approach. But good luck to those who witness on the streets for the Lord.

When Mervyn had asked me to join the evangelisation team at Elim, I agreed, but after a few times standing on a triangular traffic island at the Bakers Arms, a busy junction and shopping area in Leighton, with a crackly loudspeaker, handing out biblical tracts, I told him that it wasn't my cup of tea.

I remember on one occasion, when I was in a team of eight people, I decided to go into a shop selling jewellery to introduce myself and the church. When I walked in, the woman behind the counter gave me a steely look and started going on about me and the team making too much noise in the street. On the wall behind her I noticed a pentagram, a five-pointed star, which, I knew, symbolises occult practices. Seeing that I was getting nowhere, I said goodbye, left, and returned to the rest of the team.

'I think that woman in the shop is a witch, man,' I said to two of the team. 'We need to pray.'

As we stood there praying, the woman came outside the shop and stood there staring at us. Soon after, for whatever reason, the shop ceased trading.

But, as I said, I found that I preferred the one-to-one approach with people. Wherever I was, in a garage, a restaurant, a shop, anywhere, I'd try to introduce Jesus into the conversation. For example, I was once in an Indian take-away when a bloke I hadn't seen for ages came in to order a curry. When he asked me what I'd been up to, I gave him my testimony. He was gobsmacked. And sometimes I'd give flyers to strangers I met. One flyer, which I'd designed, depicted a row of cell doors, which were all locked, except one, and some graffiti on the wall said, 'Jesus can set you free'.

For a while, I got involved with the Victory Outreach Church in King's Cross, which had a big street ministry with drug addicts, and worked closely with Elim Pentecostal Church in Leyton.

I once went to a two-day evangelisation conference in Amsterdam with a group of outreach workers from Victory, including a guy called David Hamilton, who'd been a member of the UVF in Northern Ireland. Sonny Arguinzoni, the founder of the Victory Outreach Church, spoke at the conference. He'd been led to Jesus by Nicky Cruz, who'd been a member of a violent gang in New York in the late 1950s and early 1960s – until he met Jesus. He told his story in the book *Run Baby Run*, which has sold millions of copies since it was first published in 1968. While in Amsterdam, we went into the city's red light area to talk to drug dealers and pimps and invite them to the conference.

One of the best Christian speakers I've ever heard was Art Blajos, a former Mexican Mafia assassin, who'd been on death row. Dressed in a dark suit, black Rayban sunglasses and with slicked-back hair and a thick moustache, I thought that he still looked like a Mafia assassin. I met him when he was based for a while at the Victory Outreach Church in King's Cross.

There were some people at the Elim Pentecostal Church in Leyton who were a bit dubious about me. With my tattoos and associations with the criminal world through my boxing, they somehow couldn't reconcile me with being a Christian. That didn't worry me at all, as the image many people have of Christians is of wimps.

We held a big meeting at the church and called it 'The Christmas Story'. I designed a poster to advertise it. To make it look less churchy, I did it in the style of a fight poster, with photos of body builders and boxers and kick boxers on it. We then went out leafleting on the Chingford Hall Estate, which was well known for violence, crime and drugs. About 400 people turned up. They watched boxing demonstrations and listened to Es Kaitell, Ronnie Surridge (who reminded me of Del Boy in *Only Fools and Horses*) and I give our testimonies.

Some of the congregation at church were unhappy about having boxing demonstrations there, but Mervyn told them that if it leads people to Jesus, that's all that matters. In fact, my feeling is that Jesus may well have sparred with his disciples, or firm. Why not? They were a lively lot.

I remember when we once erected a boxing ring on a green close to a church in Canning Town. About 300 people turned up. Mark Kaylor, a former professional British and Commonwealth middleweight champion, sparred with anyone who fancied getting into the ring. The event went brilliantly.

The following Sunday, when I went to the Victory Outreach Church in Holloway Road, I went up to two guys from the outreach team and asked them if they had enjoyed the Canning Town event.

'No we didn't,' one of them replied.

'I can't see how you can evangelise through boxing,' said the other.

Both these guys were from Wales, and I felt that they didn't really understand the kind of area Canning Town was. 'Listen, what you don't realise is that many people in Canning Town are from hard families. They won't accept a wishy-washy kind of evangelism, but they understand boxing and they understand guys who get up and tell them how they were once violent or addicted to drink and drugs until they let Jesus into their lives.'

I see events like this as sowing seeds. It's great if someone gives their life to Jesus on the day, but if they don't, a seed has been planted, and it may bear fruit many years later.

Myself, Es, Ian McDowall, a body builder, and a few other blokes, some of them doormen, began meeting regularly at the snooker club to pray. Sometimes we'd pray in the office; other times sitting on seats in the boxing ring. Pastor Mervyn used to come along and explain some of the key Christian beliefs. One time, he explained to us that the healing power of Jesus was still there today, and he encouraged us to pray with people for healing.

Because more and more people in the club were asking me about Jesus, I decided to start a church there on Sunday mornings. Mervyn and the pastor at Epping Elim Church both thought this was a good idea and they said they'd support it in whatever way they could. There were some Christians, however, who thought that it was wrong to hold a service in a place where alcohol was sold.

The first time we held a service in the club we got about fifteen people there. Some were from the club, others were friends of me and Laura. Steve White played the guitar and Dave, a guy from the Epping Elim Church, led the prayers and preached. Looking around me, I felt pleased. Here were a group of people who wouldn't normally go to a church, and yet they were now singing and praying to Jesus.

After about three months, I decided to end the Sunday service, as only a handful of people were now coming along. I then started the Paradise Club in the function room on Wednesday nights. The aim was to provide local Christians with somewhere to chill out and we gave them a glass of wine. But because there were so many bookings for the function room, we had to disband the club in the end.

Laura organised a big party for my fortieth birthday. She hired a rock band called the Bleach Boys and a disco. It was terrific. We had a whole turkey, joints of beef, chicken, smoked salmon, all sorts – it was like a medieval banquet. Aunties, uncles, cousins, Jaffa, Es, Georgie Dice, Barry the Hat, Harry Curtis, Charlie Webb and lots of other friends turned up. There must have been 150 people there, and I was over the moon. At the end, Laura produced a cake in the shape of a red boxing glove.

Steve the Carpet had agreed to come to the club to measure up for a new carpet in the foyer, so when he didn't turn up, I rang him. 'Hello, mate. Everything all right?'

'I've done my back in, lifting a carpet out of the van,' he said. 'The pain's unbearable, but I made it down to open the shop.'

I felt strongly that God wanted me to pray with him. 'You need some prayer, son,' I said.

'I need a doctor – and you need a psychiatrist,' he quipped.

'You need prayer, man,' I repeated.

'Look, Al, I'm not in the mood for all that kind of talk today.'

'I'm coming down to the shop to pray with you.'

'No. I'll come up to the club.'

A short while later, Steve came to the club. I could see from the way he was limping and shuffling that he was in agony. 'The Lord's going to heal today,' I said encouragingly.

'Get on with it, Al. I've got a lot of things to do,' he said impatiently.

I placed my hand on his shoulder. 'Steve, the Lord's told me to tell you that he's going to heal you now,' I said.

He looked unimpressed, but he allowed me to carry on.

'Lord,' I prayed, closing my eyes, 'Lord, I know that I have no power; but you do. I know that you have got your hand on Steve's life, but he doesn't believe it yet. I ask you to take this pain away, in the name of Jesus. I ask you, Lord Jesus, to heal his back. Let Steve know that you alone perform miracles and that you can work them today just as you did 2,000 years ago. In Jesus' name.'

'Steve, I believe you will be 96 per cent healed straight away, and that by the morning you will be 100 per cent healed,' I said.

Clearly relieved that what I think he saw as an ordeal was over, he then left and returned to his shop. The following morning he phoned me.

'Al, I don't know what's happened, but what you did worked. All the pain's gone. As soon as I left the club, most of the pain disappeared. And then when I woke up this morning I was as right as rain.'

I smiled to myself. 'Listen, mate, I didn't do anything. It was the Lord. Jesus has healed you, as I knew he would.'

'I don't know about that, but thanks, mate, anyway.'

'Praise the Lord.'

On New Year's Eve we held a party at Haydn's, and the place was packed. Steve came up to me during the night and said, 'Alan, I've had enough of the way I'm leading my life, and I want to change,' adding after a pause, 'but I can't do it.'

I could see he'd had a few drinks. I suggested he came to church with me. He agreed, and in January 1997 I took him, and Chrissy Morris, a doorman and kick boxer, to the Way In Christian

Fellowship in Woodford, based at my old school. I wanted them to hear Jimmy Tibbs, a top boxing trainer, give his testimony. Jimmy had trained fighters such as Nigel Benn and Danny Williams.

The service was very lively. There were drums, electric guitars and singing and dancing. I could tell that it wasn't what Steve had expected.

Jimmy Tibbs then got up and gave his testimony and talked about how Jesus had changed his life. At the end of the service the pastor stood up and invited those who wanted to ask Jesus into their lives to come forward to the stage.

I looked at Steve and said, 'Do you want to go up?'

He shook his head. 'No. I want to talk to you about it afterwards, back at the snooker club.'

When we got to Haydn's I made us each a cup of coffee and we went into the office. 'You've listened to Jimmy Tibbs and, over the last three years, you've heard what I have to say. I've tried to answer all your questions,' I said.

'But I can't change on my own,' he replied.

'None of us can, mate. The only way we can change is to ask Jesus to help us. If you ask Jesus today, he'll give you a new life.'

'I want to commit my life to Jesus,' Steve said.

'Okay, let me pray with you.'

I silently prayed to the Holy Spirit for the right words to say to Steve, then said, 'Steve, we're going to pray the prayer of repentance. This is a very powerful prayer. You're going to ask Jesus to forgive you for all the sins that you have committed. You'll become born again and you'll have a fresh start.'

'I want to do this, Al.'

I then said the prayer of repentance and Steve repeated the words after me. At the end of it, I smiled at him and said, 'Your new life is beginning. Trust in Jesus from now on. They have a party in heaven when someone turns away from their old life and accepts the Lord.'

Today, Steve preaches about Jesus to thousands of people. He's also a member of Tough Talk, a group of former East End hard men who travel around giving power lifting and weight lifting demonstrations and telling how Jesus has changed their lives.

By this time, Laura and I were both starting to feel that the club was taking over our lives. Where once we had gone to church three or four times a week, now we hardly ever went. We were too busy involved in running the business. Most Saturday nights we'd have a wedding or birthday function, and we wouldn't get to bed until 3 a.m.

But I still prayed, both alone and with other people. I have to be honest and say that I also got frustrated with the church. I know it sounds bad, but I used to get bored at many of the services. A lot of the congregation probably didn't feel like this, but I did. What's more, many of the people who went to the church when I first went there had moved on elsewhere. For a while I went to the Christian Life Centre in Churchfields Road, Woodford Green.

If you stop going to church, other Christians will often ask you when they meet you, 'Have you backslidden?' This annoys me, because you don't have to go to church on a Sunday to worship Jesus Christ. The Church is important, but it's not God: it's a fellowship of God's people. You could go to church every Sunday for fifty years and not believe that Jesus Christ is who he is. For me, it's the relationship with Jesus that is most important, not a relationship with the Church.

The fruit machines were bringing in a thousand quid a week, but I'd begun to wonder if was right to have them in the club. I knew that some customers were addicted to them and they were feeding most of their wages into them. I remember a mate of mine spending the entire afternoon playing the fruit machines. He lost all his money and he was worried what he would tell his wife. On the other hand, the fruit machines paid the rent. What could I do?

By the start of 1997, things were not going well at the club. The rent had gone up to £1,500 a week and the takings were down by a couple of grand a week. Only a few people were coming in to play snooker and we were struggling to pay the bills. On top of this, there was a bad chemical smell coming into the club from the printer's below, which had started to print scratch cards. Laura and I discussed whether to keep the club open or not.

In April we finally decided to close the club. I informed the staff, paid them off, and let them take some of the signs and posters from the American bar. When I locked the door for the last time, I felt very sad. In the three years I'd run the club, we'd introduced a lot of new activities, including not only kick boxing and Thai boxing classes, but also line dancing, children's dance classes and birthday parties. And, more importantly, I had seen God at work in the three years of running the club. Steve the Carpet, Dave Lipscombe, Charlie Smith, one of the barmaids and others had given their lives to Jesus. And I had seen many healings of one sort or another.

Immediately, I began looking for a new enterprise. My solution came when I heard that the floor above a body building gym in Forest Road, Walthamstow, was available for rent. I took it, put a ring in, and opened Champions Gym. I then rented space to instructors who ran classes in boxing, kick boxing, karate, weight lifting and dancing.

I love boxing gyms. Like in snooker clubs, there's always real characters popping in and out and some great banter and camaraderie. And I love the sounds – the buzzer on the ring clock, the skipping ropes hitting the floor, the punch bags, the pads, the boxers blowing the air out of their cheeks as they shadow box – and the smells of White Horse oil and Deep Heat massage cream.

Running the gym was very hard work. I'd start at 7.30 a.m. and often not leave until 10.30 p.m. after I'd mopped the floor and cleaned out the spit buckets. I stayed there for a year.

Mickey Theo, who used to work the doors with Lenny McLean and who appeared in the film *Snatch*, asked me if I'd train Mark Potter, a young heavyweight boxer. When I sparred with Mark for the first time, I thought I might have another great white hope on my hands. I was very impressed by his power and speed.

Mark was managed by Charlie Smith, a well-known Romany gypsy who'd been a bare knuckle fighter and was now an unlicensed boxing promoter, and also a born-again Christian. Charlie applied on my behalf to the British Boxing Board of Control for a licence. Charlie was a colourful character who regularly sang in pubs and, at one time, had a band called E17 (not the boy band). He'd given his life to Jesus one afternoon in my office.

The British Boxing Board of Control called for an interview, and Charlie came along with me to their headquarters in Borough High Street. Sitting in a large mahogany-lined boardroom, with old oil paintings of prize fighters, bare knuckle boxers and the Marquis of Queensbury hanging on the walls, I was questioned by a panel of men sitting behind a large table about how I trained fighters, conditioned them, what would I do if I threw the towel in and the referee kicked it out, and how I dealt with cuts and injuries. At the end, one of the panel said it was lovely to hear a man who knew what he was talking about. I was duly granted my Professional Boxers Trainers and Seconds Licence.

I was over the moon. I remember standing on the platform at Borough tube station and seeing a poster opposite me that read, 'I can do all things through strength in Christ Jesus'. Turning to Charlie, I pointed at the poster and said, 'Exactly'.

He smiled, 'That's right, Al.'

Charlie and I went to see boxing promoter Frank Warren to see if he would put Mark Potter on one of his bills. The meeting went well and a week or so later Ernie Fossee, Frank's match maker, contacted me and said he would put Mark up against Joe Bugner Junior on the Prince Naseem bill at Wembley Arena on 19 July 1997.

My hear sank initially because both Mark and Joe were training at my gym. This would have to change, as you can't have two men who are going to fight each other training in the same gym; they'd know too much about each other's strengths and weaknesses. Surprise plays a key element in any fight. Ernie offered a purse of two grand, which was very good at the time. I knew that there were great expectations riding on Joe, but I felt confident that Mark could beat Bugner.

I was with Mark in the gym the day before the fight, and said to him, 'You know what you've got to do, son, don't you.' Mark had a pony tail, and for a boxer to go into the ring with long hair is risky, as it can fall into your eyes and obscure your vision.

He nodded. 'I'm going to get my hair cut this afternoon.'

Charlie drove Mark I and to Wembley Arena in his black Mercedes with beige leather seats. On our way there I put on a Bible tape to focus our minds on the Lord. Mark, who wasn't a Christian at this point, although I'd spoken to him about Jesus and prayed with him, was asleep in the back.

It was a great feeling as we walked through the entrance and made our way to our dressing room. I was very nervous because I was entering a world as a new kid on the block, and knew that many of the other trainers of pro fighters had been in the game for years. When I told Jimmy Tibbs of my anxieties and asked him how I should place the strips of white oxide tape between Mark's fingers (this is done so that a boxer can punch better), he replied, 'Don't worry, son. You wrap his hands the way you do in the gym.'

When Charlie and I led Mark out of the dressing room towards the arena I could hear the buzz of the crowd. Charlie and I wore blue gowns with a white trim, because Mark was a Tottenham Hotspur fan. On the back of the gowns we'd embroidered the Christian fish symbol and the words 'No weapon against you will prevail', taken from the prophet Isaiah. Chris Sanigar, a well-known and experienced pro trainer, and Keith Butler, both born-again Christians, acted as corner men.

It was a six-round fight. At the end of each round when Mark returned to the corner I prayed, 'Lord, give him strength in Jesus' name.' After three rounds Mark was ahead on points, but in the last round Joe Bugner knocked Mark down. I thought, no, this is it now. He's out.

'Get up! Get up!' I screamed at him, as the referee began the count.

He hauled himself up just in time to beat the count and immediately went back on the attack. When the referee announced that Mark had won on points, we all went crazy. It was incredible. I could spot Laura and Sean up in the balcony, standing up and shouting. When Charlie drove me home that night, I felt very proud that my hard work with Mark had paid off and he had won.

Mark Potter went on to have fourteen professional fights with me as his trainer, winning thirteen, six of those being first-round knock-outs. He also beat the record at York Hall, Bethnal Green, for the fastest knock-out. I think it was in seven seconds.

I took on another pro boxer, Patrick Passy, a former kung fu fighter who I called the 'Ice Man'. However, he stopped training and boxing and, sadly, a few years later ended up being shot dead in his car by a motorbike gunman in Edmonton.

In 1999 the British Boxing Board of Control withdrew my licence because they discovered I was promoting unlicensed boxing. I quit Champions Gym after a year and moved to the Peacock Gym in Caxton Street, Canning Town.

Located beneath Silvertown Way flyover, in the old docks area, and surrounded by factories, warehouses and derelict pubs, the Peacock is reckoned to be the best boxing gym in London – if not the country. A sign above the entrance says 'Proud as a Peacock', and on the walls of the cafeteria and reception area are signed photographs of boxers such as Mike Tyson, Prince Naseem, Nigel Benn, Billy Walker and Jimmy Tibbs.

I had now become a full-time unlicensed boxing trainer and promoter. Unlicensed boxing is an alternative to the kind of boxing you see on TV. It follows the same rules, but the fighters are not training every day; they all have day jobs. Around a third of the guys who take up unlicensed boxing are doormen. Others might be roofers or builders, for example. And some are what's known as 'chaps' – in other words, they have a reputation for being involved in some form of criminal activity.

I think the guys who get into the ring at an unlicensed boxing show do so for the buzz it gives them, and the kudos and mystique that goes with it. They like to see themselves on the posters and have people come up to them and congratulate them on their fights. The fights are just that – fights. They're more exciting and aggressive than licensed professional boxing, and it's called unlicensed because it's not licensed by the British Boxing Board of Control. But it's legal. The British Boxing Board of Control isn't a government body, as many people seem to think – it's just a private company.

Just like with pro boxing, unlicensed boxing fights have a referee, time keeper, a judge, use boxing gloves, gum shields, groin shields and, in the case of serious injuries, my shows always have two fully qualified paramedics, a doctor and a well-equipped ambulance on standby. Unlicensed boxing follows the same rules as pro boxing except fights are shorter than pro boxing and we have less of them. In unlicensed boxing we have anything from three two-minute rounds to ten two-minute rounds. For example, a world title fight in unlicensed boxing is ten two-minute rounds, while in pro boxing it's twelve three-minute rounds. With pro boxing you usually know who's going to win, as they often put up a journeyman boxer against a top boxer, and I believe this makes for boring fights. Unlicensed boxing is far more unpredictable and exciting.

One day, a guy called Craig Goldman phoned me up and told me that Channel 5 had commissioned him to make a documentary about unlicensed boxing, bare knuckle fighting and 'no holds barred wrestling'. I was wary because not long before a researcher for the *Tonight with Trevor McDonald* programme on ITV phoned me up and said that they wanted to do a feature on unlicensed boxing. I could tell that she thought it was illegal, so I explained that it was all above board and not bare knuckle fighting. A few weeks later the programme sent someone with a hidden camera to film at one of my shows. Even though there was absolutely nothing to criticise, when the programme appeared, as I expected, it presented unlicensed boxing as a murky sport with no medical supervision. This was also the way the *News of the World* wanted to present it when they contacted me on one occasion, offering money if I would talk to them about unlicensed boxing. I didn't take them up on the offer.

Craig and I met at Jefferson's Bar and Grill in Buckhurst Hill. A tall, studious-looking guy with glasses and a friendly face, he said that he'd like to film at the Last Man Standing Show at the Epping Forest Country Club in Chigwell in February 2000. This show would also feature several bouts of what's known as ultimate fighting. Ultimate fighting had arrived in Britain from the USA: it's a form of fighting where more or less anything goes. But you're not allowed to gouge eyes, head-butt or hit in the groin.

I felt that Craig was genuine and that the Lord wanted this event filmed. Some time before, Es told me that he'd had a vision of me at a televised boxing show telling people about Jesus. So I agreed to let him and a crew come along. I also invited him round to my house to view some boxing tapes, so that he'd get a clearer picture of what the show would be like.

Three weeks later a camera crew were driving up the long drive of the Epping Forest Country Club. The show was a sell-out and the crowd were buzzing with expectation, but because the club had had a bit of trouble before, I brought in Es and his team to run the doors and also installed metal detectors at the entrance.

There's a lot of stress on the evening of a show. You worry that the fighters might be ill or that they might pull out, you have to deal with the trainers, sort out tickets and money, meet VIPs and officials, and make sure that the security team know what their job is. Jamie gets the fighters out, Laura sits on the door, and Sean also helps out. Once the first two fighters come out, I sit down at a ringside table, along with the officials and VIPs. After that, I can relax a little. I always pray that my fighter wins, but I also pray that neither man gets hurt.

The Last Man Standing Show was a sell-out and a great success, and I was filmed praying with my fighters. The only downside was when a tear-up started between some unlicensed boxing and ultimate fighting fans. This happened after a trainer jumped into the ring and started pushing the referee around because he disagreed with a decision. The fans started throwing plastic glasses and chairs at one another, but Es's security boys soon sorted out the trouble-makers and ejected them from the hall.

The premiere of the film was held at a Soho wine bar, which had been hired out for the night. Laura and I were driven there in a stretch Ford Granada limousine. It was a great night, and the guests included Roy Shaw, Joey Pile, Nosher Powell, Dave Courtney and Alan Ford, who has appeared in films such as *The Long Good Friday*, *The Krays* and *Snatch*.

When the programme was broadcast on Channel 5 as *Natural Born Fighters*, it pulled in 800,000 viewers and really put unlicensed boxing on the map. The demand for tickets for the shows increased dramatically and I had more people wanting to fight. But I soon decided that ultimate fighting was not my cup of tea. I thought it was too violent and more like street fighting than sport.

Much later, Craig invited me to play the part of a minder in the film *Bulla: the Movie*, and he filmed a fight scene in the ring at one of my shows at the Circus Tavern in Purfleet, Essex. I was also interviewed by Nell McAndrew, the model who was the computer image that Lara Croft was based on, for a fifteen-part TV series on UK Horizon called *Born to Fight*. She visited the Peacock Gym and even did a bit of sparring with me. It was good fun.

When the Power House, a church in Wood Green, booked part of a Chinese restaurant in Wood Green one evening, they invited church members to bring some of their friends along for a meal and I was asked to put on a kick boxing demonstration and give my testimony.

I turned up with a young fighter, Ricky Judd, also a born-again Christian. The people with the Power House were sitting at one end of the restaurant and the regular punters at the other end.

After the meal, tables and chairs were moved back and I went with my fighter into the gents, where I put on a black vest with the Christian fish symbol on the front and a pair of tracksuit bottoms, and Ricky changed into white satin kick boxing trousers and a white satin poncho, which had 'Jesus is Lord' embroidered on the back.

In order to create the atmosphere of a kick boxing show, Ricky put on a tape which included a modern, jazzed-up version of 'Amazing Grace'. When the music started, we came out. Looking at the faces of the people from the church, I could tell that they weren't sure what to expect.

I stood in the middle of the floor and introduced myself. 'My name's Alan Mortlock. I'm a fully qualified boxing trainer and kick boxing trainer, and I've been in martial arts for thirty years. I'm here tonight to do a demonstration with Ricky, one of my boxers. But I'm also here to tell you how my life has been changed by Jesus.'

I then put on a pair of hook and jab pads on my hands, and signalled to Ricky to begin. He went through a combination of rapid moves: jabs, uppercuts, hooks, crosses. I then swapped the pads for a kick shield, a plastic shield filled with foam rubber, and he went into spinning back kicks, front kicks, side kicks, hooking kicks and roundhouse kicks. As each kick hit the shield, gasps went up in the restaurant.

At the end, everyone applauded wildly. I then invited several people from the audience to have a go at punching and kicking the pads. They really enjoyed it. After that, I gave my testimony.

I also put on a kick boxing demonstration and gave my testimony at a church in Coventry. My son Sean came with me. There must have been about 300 people in the church, a modern, octagonal building. When Sean began to kick the pads, a sound like rifle shots echoed around the church. People started stamping their feet, clapping and cheering. It was brilliant.

A feeling began to grow inside me that God was calling me to use my love of boxing to witness to the hard men and villains around East London. Because of my own background and the fact that I trained boxers, I felt I had a credibility and respect among these guys.

One afternoon, I was sitting alone in the steam room at the David Lloyd Club in Chigwell, as I often did. I prayed, 'Lord, I'm so happy with what you've done in my life. If you want me to tell the hard men, villains, drug addicts, nutcases and psychopaths I meet about you, lead me to them.' And, deep down, somehow, I knew that he would.

# 13

# The Underworld

I was travelling along East India Dock Road one wet afternoon with a mate in his forty grand Jaguar. He was a tough guy and, I knew full well, was involved in various criminal activities.

'How do you reckon things have changed on the streets since you were at it, Al?' he asked.

'It's more dangerous out on those streets nowadays, man,' I remarked, thinking of a shooting that I'd read about. 'In the old days you might get hit by a bottle or a glass or get stabbed. When I was in that tear-up outside the Room at the Top club in Ilford, none of us carried shooters. It was a major thing back then if anyone pulled a piece. But that's not the case today. Look at all the Yardie shootings in London. It's changed, mate – it's far more dangerous.'

Contrary to what you see in films, moving in what some people would call the underworld isn't glamorous and romantic. It might appear that way, but that's fiction. The blood spilt on the streets is real, and, as I discovered after that fight following my night out at the Room at the Top, a violent lifestyle can lead to you being banged up in prison. It's no fun constantly looking over your shoulder when you walk down a street, having to stand with your back to the wall every time you go into a pub or club, or peer cautiously through the window when you hear a car pull up outside. As a face once remarked, 'It's no joke ending up in the boot of a car with a bullet in your nut.'

After one of my shows, Jason Guiver, a stocky, tough-looking thirty-year-old guy, asked me if he could train with me. He'd been a very good kick boxer and he'd had his first fight at Haydn's when I ran the gym there. Jason's a born fighter and someone with a big reputation. A fearless guy who bites very easily, he's been stabbed, attacked with a baseball bat, and found himself staring down the barrel of a gun. At one time, he ran his own security company, supplying door staff to pubs. He's been involved in a few things, I should imagine, and his home's been raided by the Old Bill.

So I started training Jason at the Peacock Gym. One day, I was sitting in the reception area with him and his mate Peter, a huge, bald-headed bloke, who'd once shot himself in the neck after a row with his wife.

'You're not doing any running, son,' I said to Jason. I can always tell if a fighter's trying to moody me about his road work. Some fighters hate to run, and I could tell Jason wasn't doing any running because of his performance on the pads with me.

'I can't run,' he said, shaking his head.

'Why not?'

'I've had this terrible back problem for a couple of years.'

'Well, how about a bit of prayer, son?'

Jason gave a nervous laugh. 'What do you mean, prayer?'

'Through the power of prayer, Jesus can heal you, man. It's nothing to do with me. He just uses me as a channel.'

'Okay. When?'

'Now,' I replied.

'Now? Where?' said Jason, casting a nervous glance at Peter, who laughed.

'Outside.'

So we went outside and stood in front of the gym, which is opposite a car repair garage, and I laid one hand on his back and the other on his shoulder and asked God to heal him in Jesus's name.

Two days later he rang me and, with excitement in his voice, told me that he had just completed a four-mile run with no pain. He was absolutely bewildered and couldn't believe it.

After a training session one afternoon, Jason asked me to explain more about what I believed in. I told him that there was a heaven and a hell, and that heaven is a nice place and hell isn't. If you know Jesus Christ, you go to heaven. If you don't, you go to hell. This was brought out well in the film *Ghost*, starring Patrick Swayze, which portrayed two places where people went to after they died: a place of bright light or a place of horrible darkness.

'So what about people in my family who have died and didn't know Jesus?' he asked, furrowing his brow. 'Are you saying they're in hell?'

'No, I ain't saying they're anywhere. I'm telling you what I believe. I believe that if you don't acknowledge Jesus as Lord you can end up in hell. That's what the Bible says, and I believe the Bible is the word of God. That's all I'm saying.'

'So what do you do then?'

'You can't get into heaven by being a goody-goody or giving your money away. What you do is give your life to Jesus and he forgives you for all the things you've done wrong in the past. You don't have to have been a murderer or an armed robber to do wrong. Little old ladies who have never hurt anyone in their lives have done things wrong. The Bible teaches that all sin falls short of the glory of God.'

'How do you mean?'

'It's natural for all of us to sin. Do you teach your little baby to be bad?'

'No.'

'Do you teach your baby to be good?'

'Yeah, of course.'

'Well, why do you have to teach your baby to be good.'

He shrugged. 'I dunno.'

'Because there's natural sin as a result of Adam and Eve. You don't have to teach a child to be naughty or to lie. It's there already. You have to teach a child to be good. So when you ask Jesus into you life your old life dies and he gives you a new one.'

'What, do you believe in Adam and Eve, then?'

'Yeah. I'm not bothered about what some people say. I believe that there was a Garden of Eden and that Adam and Eve did a wrong 'un and that's how sin came into the world. Jesus is called the second Adam.'

'So do you believe in Noah's Ark?'

'Yeah. I believe they went in two by two and I believe there was a flood. That'll do me.'

He went away unsure about what I'd told him, but I'd managed to get him thinking about Jesus.

I always pray with all my fighters before they go into the ring – even if they don't believe in God. I tell them that Jesus rose from the dead, and that's why he can heal, and why people can be free from things that enslave them. Jesus is everything for me. I don't take a Christian head out of the cupboard for an hour and then put it back in again. I live each day with Jesus.

Many people take the Lord's name in vain without realising what they are saying. I understand this, but I don't like blaspheming and have my own ways of dealing with it. Often, I'll respond 'Amen'. When one of my boxers got angry and blasphemed in front of me one day, I said, 'You know a friend of mine.'

'What?' he said, looking puzzled.

'You know a friend of mine,' I repeated.

'Who?' he asked.

'Jesus.'

'What do you mean?' he replied, looking even more puzzled.

I grinned. 'Well, don't you know him? You've just said his name.'

'Oh, sorry, Al,' he said apologetically.

'No, don't say sorry. I can tell you about Jesus if you want to know him. He's a friend of mine.'

I felt the Lord wanted me to stage a meeting at the Elim Church in Leyton with boxing demonstrations and testimonies from hard men. Mervyn thought this was a great idea, so I got to work on it. I arranged for Arthur White, a former world champion power lifter, Ian McDowall, a body builder, and Steve the Carpet to give their testimonies.

I wanted to come up with a catchy name, so I prayed about it and hit on the name Godfellas, a pun on one of my favourite films, *Goodfellas*, the American gangster film starring Robert de Niro and Joe Pesci. I designed the posters in the same style as the film poster. They had the faces of Arthur, Ian and Steve on them, each dressed in a white shirt and black tie.

The church sent a team out to put the posters up in shops, community centres and other places in the area, while I delivered flyers to flats on the nearby Cathall Road Estate, which was known as 'The Bronx' because of the crack houses, violence and prostitution there.

Five hundred people turned up and the atmosphere was electric. I'd erected a boxing ring inside the church, and it was quite amusing to see little old ladies sitting with mean-looking East End hard men. Fifty people put their hands up to accept Jesus in their lives. Afterwards, I felt a great spiritual buzz, not because I was proud of what I'd done, but because I'd done the Lord's work.

The following week, I was in the Peacock Gym one morning when I overheard a group of blokes lifting weights at the far end talking about Godfellas. They'd seen an item on BBC TV about it, and I heard one of them laugh when he discovered we were all talking about Jesus.

'I was one of the Godfellas,' I shouted across to him.

He looked startled and then asked me what it was all about, so I started telling him about Jesus and ended up giving him my phone number. Although he never phoned me, I believe I maybe sowed a seed of faith. Who knows.

Roy Shaw often comes to my shows, and he's a good friend of mine. I first met him in the Villa night club in Gants Hill when his son, Gary, asked me if he could fight at one of my kick boxing shows. I call Roy 'The Legend' because, with Joey Pile, he first put unlicensed boxing on the map. When he fought Lenny McLean it made the national newspapers.

Unlicensed boxing and kick boxing attract very different crowds. Unlicensed boxing attracts a real streetwise East End and Essex crowd, who are usually suited and booted. Boxing night-outs have a long tradition in the East End and Essex.

Kick boxing, on the other hand, tends to attract more of a martial arts crowd who generally wear sports gear to the shows. Some people have a fear of going to an unlicensed boxing show; they see it as underground and worry that they might get beaten up. But I always tell them that it's perfectly safe to come along. And it is.

In the past, I've organised open-air boxing shows at the Epping Forest Country Club, held beside the swimming pool. They attracted a mixture of families, Essex wide boys, car dealers, villains and even celebrities. I remember meeting Steve McFadden, who plays Phil Mitchell in the TV soap *EastEnders*. He'd come to watch Hughy 'The Battersea Banga' Robinson fight.

In order to get more credibility with TV companies, in 2002 I set up the IBA (Independent Boxing Association), which currently has members from England, Ireland, Wales and Scotland. My aim is to license all the 300 or so boxers who fight at the shows I promote or sanction. In order to get a licence, the boxers have to undergo a medical, and produce evidence from their doctors that they are fit enough to fight. So far, around a quarter of the boxers have done this. It's a slow business, but eventually I'll get there.

I believe that there's a fighter waiting to get out in most men, but some prefer watching it to doing it. Most of the guys I train release their aggression in the ring, not in the pubs and clubs. Boxing gives them a focus and a goal. They know that they can't go out boozing or taking drugs if they're training for a fight. This makes them better people and it has a knock-on effect in the lives of their wives, girlfriends or children. And, as I've said before, many also like the buzz of a show. Jason Guiver has joked that if he could walk from the changing room to the ring every week without having to fight, he'd be quite happy.

There's a saying that it's not the size of the dog in a fight; it's the size of the fight in a dog. In other words, it's about how big your heart is. I can double a man's punching capacity in three minutes by teaching him how to put his body weight behind a punch.

I train fighters in three gyms – the Peacock in Canning Town, and the Pro Am and Bannatine's, both in Chingford – and consider myself to be good at it. In my opinion, a good trainer is someone who's always willing to listen to their boxer and let their boxer listen to the advice of people such as Jimmy Tibbs, who has a good reputation in the fight game. You have to be strict with your fighters, though, and know when a fighter has had enough.

I know that some Christians think I'm promoting violence, but I don't see boxing as violence. It's a controlled sport. Violence to me is when someone attacks someone else with a knife or a glass or shoots them. I reckon that show jumping or rugby are more dangerous sports than boxing.

In 2002 Es Kaitell set up an alternative to church, on Wednesday evenings at the offices of WK Security, his company in Forest Gate which supplies door staff to pubs and clubs, bodyguards to private individuals, and also trains door supervisors. He started these meetings because many tough guys wouldn't be comfortable going to 'normal' churches. They would see this as wimpish.

A lot of people I mix with think that going to church is boring and a waste of time, and they'd only go there for a wedding or funeral. But if you ask them if they want to go to a meeting at a security company office, not to church, they're more interested.

When we meet, we ask if anyone has any worries or any good news about what the Lord has done in their life. We pray for specific things, such as healings, and about difficulties people are experiencing in their lives; we also have Bible study and sing songs.

I was training in the gym one afternoon with Micky T, a well-known East End face who has specialised in 'debt collecting', illegally importing cigarettes, and running various unlawful commercial enterprises.

Not long before, he'd been arrested in a joint operation by the police, the Customs and Excise, and the Federation Against Copyright Theft after he was discovered to be running a major pirate video set-up, using master copies imported from the USA. He had set up one hundred video machines in a warehouse and was distributing 3,000 copies around the country. From this he was earning £12,000–£16,000 a week.

He was charged with £1.2 million VAT evasion and copyright theft, but when the case went to Wood Green Crown Court the prosecution were unable to mount a strong enough case. The VAT evasion charge was dropped and he got off with a £6,000 fine and 200 hours' community service.

A former judo fighter, he'd asked me for private boxing lessons because he wanted to keep himself in shape. Although Micky was in his early forties, he was still very lean and strong, but watching the way he punched the pads on this particular day, I could tell that he'd been hitting the charlie.

'What's the matter, Micky?'

'I'm all right, Al,' he replied unconvincingly.

'Come on. I know you're not. What's up?'

He stopped punching, went over to the bench, sat down, and put his head in his hands. 'To be honest, Al, I feel like killing myself.'

I sat down next to him. 'Why, mate?' I knew that the cocaine had a lot to do with the way he was feeling.

'I've had enough,' he said, shaking his head. 'My relationship with my girlfriend has broken up and each day I get up I feel dreadful. That's why I want to end it.'

'Look, Micky, there's only one person who can help you.'

'Who?' he said, looking me in the eye.

'Jesus, mate.' I'd told Micky about Jesus some years before and he'd been healed of a serious back problem after I'd prayed with him.

'You reckon?'

'Yeah, mate. Listen, I want you to come to a meeting Es runs at his offices in Forest Gate. It's nothing heavy.'

'Okay, then. I've nothing to lose,' he shrugged.

Micky did come with me to Es's meeting the following week, and he's been a number of times since. He's invited Jesus into his life, but he is still struggling with his faith and his criminal lifestyle. However, Micky feels that he's been able to leave the relationship with his girlfriend of thirteen years behind, something he never thought he'd be able to, as he was deeply in love with her. He feels that God has given him a new start and that his relationship with his eight-year-old daughter Jemma Jane is very strong, despite the break-up.

Micky knows that I don't judge him for some things that he may still be involved in. Jesus said 'judge not and you shall not be judged'. Micky knows that, but it can take a long time for a person to fully allow Jesus into every area of their life. And I know that Micky feels guilty about certain activities. This is a good sign; before, he wouldn't have questioned some of his activities. God loves us all, no matter how bad we might think we are. As someone once said to me, 'There's no us and them with God.'

I see a person's faith journey as similar to that of a tree shedding its leaves in autumn. The leaves don't all drop off at once. They drop off one by one. Letting go of sin is like this; we do it bit by bit. True, God will punish us if we do wrong, just as the law will, but God will still love you – although he won't have liberties taken with him. He loves the sinner, but not the sin. As it says in the Bible, 'Fear of the Lord is the first stage of wisdom.'

Just because you are a Christian doesn't mean that you don't get angry and maybe want to hit someone from time to time. When Jesus was about to be arrested in the garden of Gethsemane, one of his followers went there tooled up. He pulled out a sword and cut off the high priest's servant's ear. Jesus had words with the bloke, and then healed the servant.

I believe that if you ask God to give you self-control he will – but it's not easy, especially if you have been used to fronting it out.

For example, one night Micky T, a girlfriend of his, Laura and I went to the Dover Street Wine Bar in the West End. We hadn't been there before and we thought it sounded a classy sort of place.

As we walked down the stairs, I noticed a bloke standing at the bottom staring at Laura. When we passed him he continued to stare. What's his game? I thought, feeling anger welling up inside me. This is out of order. Part of me wanted to deck him, but another part of me said don't do it. I automatically found myself scanning the wine bar to try and work out who the bloke might be with, something I used to do in the old days when things such as this happened. Oddly, it was nearly all blokes there.

I knew that I needed a weapon: the sword of the Spirit. So I went into the gents and stood against the wall, praying silently for the strength to control my anger. 'Lord, give me the Spirit of peace and control, so that I don't lose my temper. You know I'm angry, Lord. And I give you this anger. Amen.'

Feeling calmer, I came back out to find Micky holding another bloke by the throat, up against a pillar.

'What's going on, Micky?'

'He's been staring at my girlfriend,' he said angrily.

The next minute three other guys appeared. 'Leave him alone,' said one of them.

Micky swore at them and told them to get lost. He then released his grip and faced the other three in a threatening manner. 'Do you want some, then?' he bellowed at them. But each of them backed away because they could see that he was seething with rage.

'Come on, let's go,' I said, placing my hand gently on his shoulder. 'Let's find a decent place.'

I also came close to losing it at one of my shows at York Hall in Bethnal Green. A guy from Wales had brought one of his fighters down, and from the phone conversation I'd had with him he seemed a bit mouthy and flash. What's more, I could tell that he didn't know much about the fight game.

York Hall was packed that night, but a problem occurred, though, when I discovered at the weigh-in that the guy I'd lined up to fight the Welsh bloke was about a stone too light. It turned out that when I'd booked the guy his trainer had misinformed me. Another fighter volunteered to take his place, as his opponent had failed to turn up. Even though he'd never fought before and the Welsh guy had around forty fights under his belt, he was eager.

I told the Welsh trainer, who was standing on the other side of the barrier that separates the audience from the VIP area and the ring, that the fight couldn't go ahead but that I had a replacement.

He reacted angrily. 'I'm not having this. No way.'

'What do you mean you're not having this? Your man's experienced. The other bloke's never been in the ring before.'

'No way! It's not happening.' He too was now shouting.

I'd had enough. 'Don't you talk to me like that. Who do you think you are? You don't know what you're talking about,' I screamed at him at the top of my voice. For an instant I wanted to leap over the barrier and give him a right hander, but I resisted it. The hall fell silent.

'Do you want me to sort it, Al?' asked Tiger, one of my fighters, coming up to me.

'No. Leave it,' I replied.

At the end of the show, the trainer apologised to me.

'And I apologise for shouting at you,' I said. 'But don't ever do that again. You don't know the fight game. I do.'

Driving back home after the show, I reflected on the incident and thought that I shouldn't have reacted in the way that I did. This was my old self coming back. But then I thought to myself, yeah, I should have. He didn't know what he was talking about and he was trying to make me look an idiot. In the old days, I would have just chinned him. There *is* such a thing as righteous anger.

One of the things I constantly pray for is wisdom, particularly in areas of my life that I'm weak in – and I believe the devil attacks you where you are most weak. The main thing for me is not to let the Lord down – he's my best mate.

Micky T invited me to his birthday party at a pub restaurant in

Loughton one Friday night. In the old days I'd have seen it as a good night out, but now I had to think really hard about whether I went or not. This was because I knew that there'd be a big booze-up, and I might end up drinking too much. And if this happened, the door would be open and I might start to drink regularly again. So I asked the Lord to give me wisdom. The outcome was that I didn't go.

Micky told me later that the party went on until 2 p.m. on Saturday afternoon. It started with a champagne meal in the restaurant on the Friday, then moved on to Faces night club in Gants Hill, then to Roy Shaw's house, and ended up at Micky T's house. I was glad I didn't go because I may well have joined in and gone on a bender. I like a party as much as anyone else, and in these situations it's easy to get carried away, as I know from previous experiences.

A chaplain at Ashfield Young Offenders' Institution in Pucklechurch, on the outskirts of Bristol, phoned me one day and asked if I would give a talk and boxing demonstration to the inmates. I asked Jason Guiver, who had become the unlicensed super cruiser weight world and British champion, if he'd come along with me and he agreed.

When we arrived at Ashfield we met the chaplain, an ex-football hooligan, and he took us straight to the gym. As the lads came filing in, they looked at me, wondering, no doubt, what I was all about. Some smiled; others tried to look tough.

After the boxing demonstration, Jason spoke about the time his back had been healed and I gave my testimony. At the end, I said that I'd pray with anyone who wanted me to, but the chaplain came up to me and said this would be best done in the cells – or, as he called them, the pads.

About ten lads asked to be prayed with, and the chaplain took me to the wings and directed me to the cells of the men who had asked to see me.

When I walked into the first cell there were two lads there, but only one of them had asked for prayer. 'Do you want to stand outside the cell while I pray?' the chaplain asked the lad who hadn't asked to see me.

'No, I'll stay,' he said.

'Okay,' I said, sitting down on the lower bunk. 'What can I do for you?' I said to the other lad.

'I've had enough of the way my life is, but I don't know how to change it.'

'You can't change on your own, but Jesus can change you. Do you want Jesus to come into your life?' I asked him.

'Yeah, mate,' he replied.

I then prayed with him and asked him to recite the prayer of repentance with me. At this point the other lad said that he too wanted Jesus to come into his life. I went from cell to cell, doing the same thing, and each of the ten lads gave his life to Jesus; I was on the wings for about three hours. Then the chaplain told me there was another lad who wanted me to pray with him. For some reason or other, the screw wouldn't open the cell door.

'Do you want me to pray with you, man?' I asked, pressing my face to the cell door.

'Yeah,' said a voice.

'Do you want to give your life to Jesus?'

'Yeah.'

I then shouted the prayer of repentance through the door and he then repeated it.

Afterwards, the chaplain came up to me, shaking his head. 'I've never seen anything like it.'

'The power of God is moving through this prison,' I told him.

'I'm sorry I've kept you so long,' he apologised.

'It doesn't matter. This is the work of the Lord. I'd stay here all day if necessary.'

When Jason and I walked out of Ashfield, I was buzzing. I felt I'd done a good day's work for the Lord. Jason, on the other hand, was upset by the plight of the young lads, many of whom seemed to be there for relatively minor offences, such as nicking cars. He told me that he had a lump in his throat when one lad said that all he wanted Jesus to do was to help him sleep at night. It turned out that he'd crashed his car while taking his pregnant girlfriend to hospital, and both she and the unborn baby had been killed. I think God was showing Jason the inside of a prison and many other things as well.

Around this time, Jason and Micky T came with me to Wood Hill high security prison in Milton Keynes to visit Manny 'The Maniac' Clark. A stocky bloke with a shaved head and tattoos, Manny made a name for himself as an enforcer for certain faces in and around the East End. He had a reputation for extreme violence and would be frequently hired to carry out 'debt collecting'.

I first got to know him when he phoned me up one day and asked if he could box for me. I immediately agreed, as I knew he loved a tear-up. As I got to know him better over the next few weeks, I started to tell him about Jesus.

After being charged with attempted murder when a man was shot twice in the head and once in the shoulder, Manny was put on remand and sent to Wood Hill. We started writing to each other. I'd explain why he needed to accept Jesus into his life, and he would write poems for me and tell me his views about God. He told me he was praying and was close to becoming a Christian, but he was worried that some people might think he was soft, and he was concerned about what he would do if he found himself in a situation where he felt he had to defend himself.

Jason drove us to Wood Hill in his metallic midnight-blue Range Rover, which has tinted windows, TVs, DVDs and computers on the head rests of the front seats, satellite navigation and a personalised number plate.

As we parked in the car park at Wood Hill, a large, square, modern prison, I thanked the Lord that he had entered my life. If he hadn't, I might well have ended up back behind bars. The prison operates a rigorous security process. When you arrive at the visitors' centre, a small building, separate from the prison, you have to empty your pockets and place your belongings in a locker and then wait for your number to be called. You then make your way towards the prison. When you reach the entrance for the visitors you have to remove your shoes and belt and then pass through an X-ray machine. After that, you are searched by a screw and then filtered into the visiting room. In the far corner I spotted Manny, and he grinned and waved.

I went over to him, while Micky and Jason went to the snack bar to buy teas and biscuits.

'So, how's it going, mate?' I said as I sat down.

'Surviving, Al. You have to,' he replied glumly.

Jason and Micky returned from the tea bar loaded up with chocolate bars, baguettes and mugs of tea. We then talked about various people we all knew and how Manny's case was progressing – he wasn't that optimistic about getting off when the case went to trial. As we chatted, various people who were visiting other inmates came up to Manny to say hello.

After a while, Jason said to Manny, 'I'm going to be born again.' He may have said it with a smile, but I knew that God was already working in him.

'Are you joking or do you mean that, son?' asked Manny.

'No. I mean it.'

On the way back to London, both Jason and Micky T's mobiles were constantly ringing. As soon as one call ended, the phone rang again. I heard Micky say slowly in a menacing voice to someone, 'You owe me. You've got to pay. I want my money.' I could see how irate and stressed both of them were getting, and I thought to myself, I'm so glad I'm out of this game. This is no life.

Manny was eventually released from prison and in October 2002 he came along to the Wednesday evening meeting at Es's security firm. All of a sudden he said out loud, 'Thank you, Lord. Thank you for all you've done for me while I was in prison and since I've been out. I know that you've been with me.'

Es turned to Manny and said, 'Manny, I'm going to be bold here. Do you want to give your life to Jesus?'

'Yeah,' he said. 'I've had enough of the way my life has been. I don't want to carry on like this. I want a new life.'

I then prayed with Manny. He said the prayer of repentance, and I led him to the Lord.

A week later, Jason also came to the Wednesday evening meeting and gave his life to Jesus. I knew that he would, but it had to be when he felt ready. He'd already had the words 'Jesus is Lord' embroidered on his gown and poncho and a cross tattooed on his arm.

In the middle of the meeting Manny said he'd something to share, and he went on to tell how he'd been in a pub in Ruislip a few nights before with his family when a bloke at the bar racially insulted him. Manny is mixed race. Before he found Jesus, he'd have torn into him, but he didn't. However, as he was leaving the pub he gave the geezer a left hook.

'Do you think I'm going backwards?' he asked Es with a worried look.

'No, Manny. You're not going backwards,' Es replied.

'You sure?'

'Yeah. Before, you'd have probably put the bloke in hospital!'

Driving back home to Leyton later that evening, I thought about how incredible it was that guys such as Micky T, Manny and Jason had invited Jesus into their lives. They no longer see him as a painting of a man with a beard and long hair, but as someone who is real and powerful. They're now walking with the Lord and allowing him in faith to change their lifestyles. With me, that change was quite dramatic and sudden, a bit like St Paul on the road to Damascus. A phrase I saw on a T-shirt a few years ago sums it all up: 'Perfect man under construction'. And Jesus Christ is the only perfect man.

# Epilogue

Painted above the front door of Alan's house in a terraced street in Leyton, East London, are the words 'Jesus is Lord'. When you walk into the hallway the first thing you see is a two foot six statue of Mike Tyson, which was given to him by Roy Shaw. These two things tell you that here lives a man who is passionate about God and passionate about boxing.

He's also passionate about his family. During the eight months we worked on the book, his wife, Laura, would always be on hand with mugs of tea and sandwiches, while from time to time his four sons would stick their heads around the door, no doubt wondering what exactly their dad was doing.

As I sat with Alan in his living room, digging into his past, his memories and feelings, his mobile or land line would often ring, and usually it would be a punter wanting tickets for a show, or one of his fighters. Alan would usually then apologise, and disappear briefly into his small office, from where he runs his shows and the Independent Boxing Association (IBA).

On the walls of the office are framed A5 flyers from some of his shows (given to him as a birthday present by his son Sean), his matchmaking board, listing fighters and prize money (between £300–£600), and a large wooden board depicting two figures of boxers in the ring and with the words 'Billy's Boxing Booth. £5 to any man who endures. Three min rounds or k. o. £100 prize money' written on it. There's also a framed article from the *Observer* from November 2001. The headline read 'Seconds Out. God's the Final Referee', and the sub-headline describes Alan as the 'Pirate Promoter'.

But at other times, someone would ring to tell Alan that they would be coming to the Wednesday evening meeting at Es Kaitell's security company, and Alan would often end the call by saying, 'Praise the Lord, mate.'

When I started writing this book with Alan, I wasn't fully aware of what a dramatic change his life has gone through, how deep his faith is, and the respect in which he is held by many hard men in and around east London. As a somewhat wavering and not very good Roman Catholic, I have to admit that I am always, at first, a little sceptical of those who claim to have the so-called 'born-again' experience. But as I listened to Alan recount his life story, and the way in which he felt God change him from the inside, I could not help but be impressed and challenged. It's hard to argue with someone who has undergone such an extra-ordinary life change and who genuinely tries to live out his Christianity day by day, while at the same time honestly acknow-ledging his weaknesses and shortcomings. Furthermore, he accepts the people he meets for who they are, irrespective of what they might or might not have done, or be doing. However, before we completed the book, I decided to ask Alan a series of questions that I thought you, the readers, might still have in the back of your minds.

*GW* As a Christian, do you feel that you have a special purpose?
*AM* I see my job as evangelising, or sowing seeds. I'm not a biblical scholar or theologian. I leave that to others, better qualified than me. I believe that God has called me to tell people about Jesus, but I'm not a discipler. This needs someone who has more time and patience than me. Put it another way. You could have a boxing

trainer, but he might not make a very good promoter. As St Paul says in his letter to the Ephesians, God has given us gifts. Some of us are called to be apostles, some prophets, some evangelists, some pastors, and some teachers. My spiritual gift is to be an evangelist. I'm on the Lord's firm. Some Christians are there to plant the seeds and some are there to water them. I'm there to plant them. And it may take a long time for the seeds to bear fruit – it took Steve the Carpet three years to give his life to Jesus.

When I gave my life to Jesus, I believe that God gave me the job of trying to reach people who wouldn't normally listen to someone talking about Christianity. This is what Mervyn Tilley told me would happen that time I went to see him soon after becoming a Christian. When that bloke gave me that Christian tract when I was walking down High Road in Leyton I just walked on. I thought Christianity was rubbish and for wimps.

My ministry is with the people who think they are furthest away from God. Guys such as Micky T, Manny and Jason will listen to me when I talk about the Lord Jesus because before he came into my life I was very much like them. And they know I wouldn't wind them up. These guys are my friends and, like me, perfect men under construction. I'll never Bible bash them. If they want to listen to what I have to say, I'll tell them. If they don't, I won't. It's as simple as that.


*GW* What about Jesus' command to turn the other cheek? How easy is it for someone like you?
*AM* I try and follow this command of Jesus, but, at times, it's not easy, I admit. For example, I once lent some money to a guy who was in a spot of trouble. I didn't know him that well, but he assured me he'd pay it back in a few weeks. However, the weeks came and went, and there was no sign of the money. I spoke to him and he eventually gave me half the money. Soon after, he asked me for another loan. I agreed, believing that I'd get both loans back, but I only got half back. I felt annoyed at this, as he didn't keep his word. He was taking liberties with me, and I don't

allow anyone to do that. So one evening I went to see him at his house. I said firmly, 'I want my money. Just because I'm a born-again Christian doesn't mean I was born yesterday.' I've never believed that Jesus wants us to be mugs. Part of me wanted to get heavy with him, but I knew this would be wrong, so I gave it to the Lord. I prayed, 'Lord, I don't want to even think like this. I ask that you sort it out and that I get my money back.' The next day, the guy did give me the money back. I have to be honest and say that I don't really know what I'd have done if he'd knocked me for the money.

And there was another time when someone was causing trouble in my family. Laura and I had to go and see this person on our way to a restaurant where we were meeting some friends for a meal. The person started insulting us both and slagging off a member of my family. Afterwards, driving to the restaurant, my blood was boiling, and I found myself swearing out loud. Then I felt the Holy Spirit telling me to stop, so I pulled the car over, got out, and stood by the road and repented out loud. I knew that the devil was trying to ruin our night out. After that, the anger disappeared and we had a great evening.

*GW* How easy is it to live as a Christian?
*AM* It's not easy, especially in the world we live in today. One time, while I was running Haydn's, I opened my Bible and found myself reading Revelation 2:2–6 (New Living Translation):

I know all the things you do. I have seen your hard work and your patient endurance. I know you don't tolerate evil people. You have examined the claims of those who say they are apostles but are not. You have discovered they are liars. You have patiently suffered for me without quitting. But I have this complaint against you. You don't love me or each other as you did at first! Look how far you have fallen from your first love! Turn back to me again and work as you did at first. If you don't, I will remove your lampstand from its place among

> the churches. But there is this about you that is good: you
> hate the deeds of the immoral Nicolaitans, just as I do.

I knew God was pulling me up and telling me that I'd become too
wrapped up in things that didn't matter. He was saying that he was
happy with the work that I'd been doing, but I wasn't putting him
and it first any longer.

*GW* Given the world that you move in, it must be hard to stay on
the straight and narrow at times.

*AM* It can be. I remember being in Loughton once with Laura
when she saw a really nice pair of trousers in a clothes shop. I said
I'd buy them for her, but she wouldn't let me because they were
three hundred quid. So I rang a good mate of mine to see if he
could get the same make any cheaper. When he came to train with
me at the gym he told me he could get two pairs for seventy quid
each. When he said this, I thought to myself that they were probably
knocked off, but I didn't want to offend him by saying this. On the
other hand, I felt the Holy Spirit telling me not to lie to him. So I
came out with it and asked, 'Are they nicked?' When he laughed
and said that they were, I told him I couldn't take them. I know I
did the right thing and I think, in a way, it strengthened my
testimony with him. The question I have to always ask myself at
times like this is: how would the Lord handle it? In the Bible it says
that you have to be as wise as a serpent and as gentle as a dove. And
I believe that.

*GW* Some Christians are against boxing because they see it as
violence. It's interesting that you don't see it this way.

*AM* That's right. I see boxing as a sport, not violence. Unlicensed
boxing is controlled and, as with professional boxing, we have a
doctor, paramedics and an ambulance at all the shows. Some years
ago, I remember reading a list of the most dangerous sports. Rugby
came out top, while boxing was twelfth. And in the gospel Jesus
said to a Roman centurion, a commander of a hundred soldiers,

and someone who must have loved a tear-up, that he hadn't come across anyone in Israel with as much faith as him.

*GW* When I went to a show you sanctioned at the Circus Tavern in Purfleet, I felt that I was entering a sub-culture.
*AM* I hadn't thought of it as a sub-culture, but, yeah, maybe it is. As I've said before, there's a strong tradition of boxing in the East End and Essex. People love to go for a night out to a boxing show. They can have a drink, a meal, meet friends and see some exciting fights. And I make my shows very entertaining. I suppose there's a touch of showbiz and razzmatazz about them.

*GW* Because of your involvement in unlicensed boxing you must meet some of London's major criminals?
*AM* I meet all sorts of people. Yeah, I know that individuals from major firms and families come to my shows, and some of them are good friends. I don't think of them as villains or gangsters.

*GW* Does it cause you any moral dilemmas when you know that some people might be involved in serious crime?
*AM* No. I accept people no matter who they are or what they've done. I'm not there to judge anybody, and I don't get involved in criminal activity any longer. These guys know that I'm walking with the Lord.

*GW* Why have you always had this fascination with fighting?
*AM* Ever since I was a kid I'd always loved anything to do with fighting, and all four of my sons have boxed or kick boxed at one time or another. I used to love playing with toy soldiers, and when I was eight I used to regularly have stone fights with the boy who lived across the road. When I first started martial arts, I immediately liked the challenge and discipline involved. Even today, I still spar regularly in the ring, either with Ian Wilson and Terry Rummell, both unlicensed boxers, Gary Bedford, a former amateur boxer, or my mate Dave Lipscombe. And I regularly train with Red Brennan,

an ex-pro boxer in his late sixties. Put it this way: some people like football or stamp collecting, for example, and I like fighting.

*GW* What's your attitude to drugs now?

*AM* I've taken five kinds of drugs in my life: alcohol, nicotine, speed, cannabis and cocaine. All drugs change your perception and thinking. Without a doubt, the one that really took the greatest grip on my life was alcohol, and I believe that alcohol was largely responsible for the death of my mum at a comparatively young age. When I snorted speed for the first time, at the age of seventeen, little did I know that I'd be a prisoner to it for the next seventeen years. I was addicted, but not in the same way that someone would be addicted to heroin. I used it as a recreational drug.

I believe all drugs are addictive. Some people argue that cannabis should be legalised, but if this happens, other drugs will be legalised. All types of drugs can lead to an early death. I know this because several friends of mine have died because of their heroin addiction or drug-related incidents. In the past, drugs gave me a buzz, but the buzz I get from working for the Lord is a hundred times better.

*GW* And what about alcohol? Do you ever have a drink now?

*AM* When I go out now, I might have a couple of bottles of lager, or if Laura and I go to a restaurant for a meal, we might share a bottle of wine. Alternatively, I might just drink orange juice or sparkling water with lime.

But I have to be honest and admit that I've lost it a couple of times. One time after a boxing show at The Circus Tavern in 2001, I ended up knocking back six pints of lager at the bar. The following morning, when I woke up, all I could think of was the old days when I virtually lived in pubs. I repented and asked the Lord for strength to resist the temptation to drink excessively. As a Christian, you constantly have to be on guard against temptation, because, as the Bible tells us, the devil is like a roaring lion waiting to devour us.

*GW* Some Christians are totally against alcohol though, aren't they? Yet the first miracle Jesus performed was when he turned water into wine at the wedding in Cana.

*AM* I don't think he turned the water into wine so that everyone could have a right booze-up. The Bible doesn't say don't drink; it says don't get drunk. You can have a couple of drinks and feel happy, but if you drink and drink the happiness disappears and it turns into a nightmare. As my dad used to say, 'When the drink is in; the wits are out.' It's a case of everything in moderation.

*GW* How do you explain the fact that when people ask God to heal them, he doesn't always do this?

*AM* I agree. God doesn't always heal when you ask him to. For example, I've asked him to heal Laura's diabetes, but he hasn't yet. I asked him to heal the ear of Paul Kavanagh, known as 'The White Destroyer', so that he could become a professional boxer. And he didn't. Yet he healed Terry Rummell's kidney stone problem.

I don't know why this is. And, I've got to be honest and admit that, at times, I've questioned God for not healing someone. Because he's my father, my brother and friend, I can ask him why some people are healed and others aren't. Yet at the end of the day, I have to accept that God's the guv'nor and his ways are not always man's ways.

I look at it this way. I've got four sons and at different times in their lives they've asked me for various things. But I've not always given them what they wanted when they wanted it. Sometimes they haven't been ready to receive what they asked for. Jesus tells us that whatever you ask for in his name you shall be given. It might not happen when you want it to, but it will happen eventually. Jesus says that no father would hand his son a stone when he asked for bread, or a snake when he asked for fish. Therefore God will give only good things to those who ask.

*GW* Do you think you would have still become a Christian if you hadn't had that strange experience that night as you lay in bed, following Steve White's visit?

*AM* No way. I'd never have become a Christian. Because of the kind of life I'd led, I think I needed that knock-out punch from God. My heart had become hard. I know that some people will be sceptical about what I say I saw that night, but I know what happened.

*GM* You must meet people who are not persuaded by your experience of God.

*AM* Yeah. I get people who say, 'Well, it's all right for you, but it's not for me. I don't need Jesus.' If they say this, I just pray for them. At the end of the day, God gave us all free will. If someone like me had talked to me about Jesus when I was getting into tear-ups and on the gear, I know I wouldn't have listened to them. For example, when I first heard that Steve White had given his life to Jesus, it made no impression on me.

*GW* To many people, the term 'born-again Christian' conjures up images of images of happy-clappy types. What do you mean when you describe yourself as 'born again'?

*AM* I suppose that some people do have negative images about 'born-again' Christians; I probably did before I gave my life to the Lord. But in John 3:3 Jesus says, 'Unless you be born again you cannot see the kingdom of God.' So, because we're so happy that we're born again, we sing lively songs and shout that Jesus is Lord. What you might call a traditional church would not have attracted me when I first became a Christian. I'd have found it too boring.

*GW* Where do you go to church now?

*AM* I go to the Wednesday evening meeting at Es Kaitell's security company in Forest Gate, but I still see the Elim Pentecostal Church in Leyton as my spiritual home. This, though, is because of the pastor, Mervyn Tilley, not the building. The Church is not the building. Jesus said where two or three are gathered, he is in their midst. But I would say that as a new Christian you do need the support of a strong Christian church to nurture you.

*GW* So, how do you perceive Jesus?
*AM* I don't see Jesus in a physical sense. I see him as the supernatural force that has created the world and mankind. I know I can rely on him, and even though I can't see him, I know that he's real and he's there. If he was walking the earth today, he'd be wise, loving, hard but fair, and a leader of men. A real proper geezer. He'd mix with the outcasts and sinners, just as he mixed with tax collectors, prostitutes and soldiers 2,000 years ago in Galilee. He said that he didn't come to call the upright, but sinners. And Jesus was no mug. When the money lenders were taking a liberty in the temple, which he called his Father's house, he drove them out with a whip.

*GW* How does God speak to you?
*AM* He doesn't speak to me with claps of thunder and a booming voice. He speaks to me through other people and everyday situations. But you have to be tuned in through prayer, reading the Bible, and fellowship with other believers to hear him.

*GW* What about the devil?
*AM* The devil is real – don't let people tell you he's not. He's the great deceiver and the enemy of God. In the Bible it says that the road to destruction is wide and the road to eternal life narrow.

When I look back to my childhood, I now think that my mum's alcoholism was something to do with the occult practices – the Ouija boards, seances, spiritualism – that she sometimes got involved in. And I think that the violence and alcoholism that marked much of my life was possibly due to a demonic influence. What's more, I know that the devil was trying to destroy my marriage through drink, and he was making a good job of it until Jesus stepped in.

There's a spiritual cosmic battle raging for the souls of mankind; and, like in any battle, you have to put on your armour. My son

Jamie works as an assistant manager and door supervisor for Es's security company. When he leaves to go to work, I always say, 'Jay, I pray for the blood of Jesus to cover you tonight.' When I'm working at home, I often have a twenty-four hour Bible digital radio channel on, so that the house is filled with the word of God. The only weapons I use now are the blood of Jesus, the Bible and prayer.

*GW* What do you think heaven is like?
*AM* I don't see heaven as a set of pearly gates and people playing harps. To me, heaven is a spiritual dimension that runs parallel with the world we live in.

*GW* How do you pray?
*AM* Prayer is very important for a Christian. If you don't talk to God, then it's difficult to have a good relationship with him. This is the same with family or friends. Some people pray for, say, an hour a day at a particular time. I used to do this, but now I don't. I pray as my heart leads me. I might be driving the car, training in the gym, or at one of my boxing shows. I pray any time, anywhere, any place.

*GW* And what about the Bible?
*AM* Reading the Bible is also key in the Christian life, because the Bible is the word of God. I find spiritual food in the Bible. If I meet someone and they want to know more about Jesus, I'll encourage them to read the Gospels first and look at what Jesus said and did. I also find a book called *Every Day with Jesus* useful. It provides spiritual reflections on Bible passages for each day of the year. Once someone has become familiar with Jesus in the New Testament, then I'd suggest that they read the Old Testament, perhaps starting with Genesis and the account of how God created the world. The Bible is full of colourful characters. For example, Moses was a murderer and David was an adulterer, yet Moses and David played key roles in God's plan to save the world. God can work through

anyone, even murderers and adulterers. As I've said before, there's no us and them with God.

*GW* Why do you think so many people in Britain today show no interest in Christianity?

*AM* When I gave my life to Jesus that evening with Steve White in December 1990, I'd no intention of becoming a Christian. I wasn't looking for God; I didn't even believe in God. I was only doing it so that Laura wouldn't leave me. But, looking back, maybe my spirit was crying out to God. I think that was why I cried out to God when I was walking through that graveyard in Walthamstow with John Hawkins. And it's funny that when I was a teenager and I used to sometimes go with my mates into churches around Woodford Bridge to disrupt services, I never felt quite right about it.

Some people claim Christianity is responsible for wars and all sorts of things, but this is not Christianity. This is man using Christianity for his own ends. For me, Christianity is not the Church, or a set of rules, it's the person of Jesus Christ, who can dramatically change people's lives. In other words, Christianity is about being Christ-like.

*GW* How relevant are the Ten Commandments today?

*AM* I see the Ten Commandments as a rule book to help you lead a peaceful life. God introduced them for our own good. If you try and stick to them, they'll keep you in the best condition, spiritually, mentally and physically, just in the same way as if a boxer follows his training programme, he'll be in tip-top condition. If you think about it, what good does it do to get off our nuts or have affairs? These things provide a temporary buzz and don't bring lasting happiness. They leave you feeling empty. If you want to know how to live, follow the maker's instructions.

*GW* The way you lead people to Jesus sounds very simple.

*AM* Yeah. When someone says that they want Jesus to come into their life, I first of all explain that they are going to be born again and then I say a prayer to the Holy Spirit to give me the right words to lead a person to Jesus. The Holy Spirit is the teacher, helper and power of the Trinity. I then ask the person to recite after me the prayer of repentance.

*GW* So what's your final message to anyone reading this book?
*AM* It's this. It doesn't matter what you are doing, have done, not done or going to do, but if you're looking for a change in your life, then you need Jesus. I know he's the only person who can sort you out. In the twelve years since I've been a Christian he's never let me down. He might make me wait for things, but he's never let me down. You don't have to go into a church to find Jesus; you can pray to him anywhere. If you speak to him, he'll hear you and, if you ask him, he'll come into your life. He said in the gospel, 'Knock and the door shall be opened. Seek and you shall find.' I hope that this book will encourage people to think about the reality of Jesus and invite him into their lives. And for those who are already Christians, I hope that they might feel inspired to make a deeper commitment to the Lord. We're all on a journey to God, and are just passing through this life on earth. We all fail and sin, but God forgives us because he loves us.